Praise for the Novels of
J.L. Abramo

CROSSING
THE CHICKEN

ALSO BY J. L. ABRAMO

Jake Diamond Mysteries
Catching Water in a Net
Clutching at Straws
Counting to Infinity
Circling the Runway

A Jimmy Pigeon Novel
Chasing Charlie Chan
(featuring Jake Diamond)

Sixty-First Precinct Novels
Gravesend
Coney Island Avenue

Nick Ventura Mysteries
Brooklyn Justice

Stand Alone Novels
American History

J. L. ABRAMO

CROSSING THE CHICKEN

A Jake Diamond Mystery

DOWN & OUT
BOOKS

Down & Out Books
3959 Van Dyke Road, Suite 265
Lutz, FL 33558
DownAndOutBooks.com

The characters and events in this book are fictitious. Any similarity to real persons, living or dead, is coincidental and not intended by the author.

Cover design by Zach McCain

ISBN: 1-64396-030-X
ISBN-13: 978-1-64396-030-2

*Dedicated to the Private Eye Writers of America
for the honor of the Best First Private Eye Novel Award,
the Shamus Award,
and the privilege of serving as President*

CAST OF CHARACTERS

Vinnie "Strings" Stradivarius. . . . . .a luckless gamble

William "Big Bill" Conway. . . . . .bookmaker and bar owner

Bobby Lockhart. . . . . .a bad bet

Frederick Hanover. . . . . .a businessman

Jake Diamond. .private investigator

Sargeant Roxton Johnson. . . . . .an SFPD detective

Darlene Roman. . . . . .Diamond's associate

Tug Mcgraw. . . . . .a loyal canine

Frances Stradivarius. . . . . .Vinnie's mother

Captain Laura Lopez. . . . . .San Francisco Police Department

Rachel Palmer. . . . . .a waitress at The Homestead

Tony Carlucci. . . . . .a *wise-guy* and restaurant owner

Josephine Leone. .a troubled mother

Jennifer Hanover. . . . . .Frederick Hanover's daughter

Nicolai Roman. . . . . .Darlene's father

Loretta Bailey. . . . . .a paid assassin

Molly. . . . . .a receptionist

Jefferson Talbot. . .a businessman, partner of Frederick Hanover

Tom Romano. . . . . .a private investigator

Mary Falco Diamond. .Jake's mother

Lionel Katz. . . . . .the Carlucci *family* mouthpiece

Margaret Lockhart. . . . . .Bobby Lockhart's mother

Sonny Badalamenti. .a friend in deed

Irving Sulam. . . . . .a notary

Edward Salerno. .a Chicago lawyer

VINNIE

My worst habit is bad luck.
—Vinnie "Strings" Stradivarius

SATURDAY

"Vinnie. Vinnie. Vinnie."

Vinnie Strings would have rather been sitting on a bed of hot coals than sitting face-to-face with William Conway across Big Bill's oak desk in the back office of the Blarney Stone Saloon.

"I know," Vinnie said.

"You knowing isn't doing you much good, and it does me no good at all. And don't insult me by telling me you are *working on it*. You have witnessed how I make examples of those who fail to pay what they owe. You know I will have no choice but to make an example of you. I didn't twist your arm to put down bets with me, but both your arms will be twisted until they snap if you can't cover your loses. I have a reputation to uphold. You may want to ask your guardian angel to bail you out again. I heard he squared your debt to Sandoval, and I heard Manny's two gorillas are still on crutches."

"I didn't ask him to do that."

"Whatever you say. In any case, do Jake Diamond a favor and explain to him that I am *not* Manny Sandoval and I don't employ morons."

"Can you give me more time?"

"Of course, Vinnie, that's why you're sitting here and not in traction at Saint Francis Memorial Hospital. One week. Go."

. . .

3

Vinnie Strings sat alone in a booth at The Homestead on 19th Street and Folsom, working on his third gin and tonic.

He was staring at the phonebooth just inside the front door.

Vinnie had come close, a few times, to leaving the table to phone Jake Diamond.

He knew Jake would help him, but not without a lecture. Vinnie decided the lecture from Big Bill had been enough for one day.

He turned his attention back to his drink, found the glass empty, and called to Rachel for another.

Minutes later, Vinnie was about to ask Rachel why she had delivered *two* drinks when Bobby Lockhart sat at the booth.

"On me," Lockhart said.

"Thanks."

Bobby and Vinnie sat in at the same poker game twice a month. They were not exactly bosom buddies, but they got along.

"I hear you're into Big Bill Conway for three large."

"Did you read about it in the *Chronicle*?"

"You know how word gets around among gamblers, we all love hearing about someone less lucky."

"I'm all right."

"You don't look all right."

"No offense, Bobby, but I would rather talk about the weather."

"I can help you."

"Why would you want to do that?"

"Because you would be helping me."

"I'll listen," Vinnie said.

"There's a cat owes me fifteen grand for work I did for him, and he's late. He said he would have the cash for me tonight—but he's said it before."

"And?"

"I told him I would drop by his house to pick it up, but I wouldn't be alone. You always look more serious when you bring someone along. I will give you twenty percent just for keeping me company. It's enough to get Big Bill off your back."

"What time tonight?"

"I can pick you up outside your place at nine."

Vinnie Stradivarius looked over to the phonebooth, and then back to Lockhart.

"Nine it is," Vinnie said.

The house was in the Richmond.

Lockhart parked on the next street and they walked.

At the front door, Bobby pushed the doorbell.

It rang the first eight notes of Beethoven's Fifth.

The man who opened the door looked at both visitors.

"Good evening, Fred," Bobby said.

"It's Frederick. What do you want?"

A gun appeared in Bobby's hand.

"You can invite us in. Fred."

The man backed away, and Lockhart stepped through the door.

Vinnie stood planted at the threshold. Confused.

"Come on," Bobby said, "and close it behind you."

"If you want money, I have around twelve hundred dollars in my wallet," Frederick Hanover said.

"Impressive," Bobby said. "Do you have a gun?"

"In my desk drawer."

"Show me."

They followed Hanover into an office at the back of the house.

"Top drawer, left side."

"Sit. Take it out, slowly. Place it on the desk, and put your hands behind your head."

When Hanover complied, Bobby handed *his* weapon to Vinnie.

"Keep him covered until I get his gun."

Bobby walked over to the desk, picked up the weapon, turned, shot Vinnie in the chest, and placed the gun back down on the desk.

"Are you insane," Hanover said.

"You have no idea."

Lockhart walked over and picked up his gun where Vinnie had dropped it when he went down. Bobby pointed the gun at Hanover.

"I'll give you a chance," Lockhart said. "I'll let you go for your weapon."

Hanover grabbed for his gun. Bobby put a bullet in Fred's head.

Bobby touched the weapon to Vinnie's hand, and placed it on the floor next to Vinnie's body.

He started out of the room, but stopped short at the door.

He walked back to the desk and lifted the small statuette.

It was a figure of a winged-woman, made in metal, six inches tall.

She stood on a green stone pedestal.

Bobby slipped it into his jacket pocket. He couldn't resist.

Lockhart had a thing for angels.

After a dinner of leftover Chinese take-out, another terrible Steven Seagal film on TV, and two chapters of Dicken's *David Copperfield*, Jake Diamond was ready to call it a night when his doorbell rang.

Jake found Detective Sergeant Johnson standing on the front porch.

"I'm just going to say it."

"Okay."

"Vincent Stradivarius was shot. An hour ago."

"Is he alive?"

"He's alive, but he may not make it."

"Where is he?"

"Saint Francis, but he'll be in surgery for hours."

"So, there's no need to rush down there."

"None I can think of."

"Care for a drink?" Diamond asked.

"Sure, I could handle a drink."

BOBBY

Every murderer is probably someone's old friend.
—Agatha Christie

1

After Sergeant Johnson gave me the news about Vinnie Strings, I invited him in for a drink.

He followed me back to the kitchen, where I poured two glasses of George Dickel Tennessee sour mash over ice.

We sat at the kitchen table.

"Has his mother been told?" I asked.

"I called Ray Boyle down in Los Angeles. He said he would personally go over to see her tonight, and book her a flight for tomorrow morning."

"Thanks for taking care of that."

"No problem."

"So, what happened?"

"I can tell you what it looked like."

"Okay."

"Vinnie and Frederick Hanover were both found in Hanover's study, a house in the Richmond. It appears there was an exchange of gunfire. Both were hit once. Vinnie was found on the floor in front of the desk, Hanover's body was behind the desk. Hanover was DOA. Guns were found near each body."

"Who was Hanover?"

"Big time businessman. Real estate developer. Obscenely wealthy. It's being looked at as a robbery gone south."

"Not possible. Not Vinnie."

"Word has it he had worked himself into debt. Nearly three

thousand dollars."

"Vinnie would take a beating before he would point a weapon at anyone. Who does he owe the money to?"

"William Conway."

"I guess I'll have to talk with Conway."

"Big Bill is a nasty piece of work. I'm just saying. Try to be polite."

"Dealing with Conway will be a walk in the park compared to giving Darlene the news."

"It's after midnight. Why don't you wait until morning to call her?"

"I will, and I'll need to tell her in person. I'm going to head over to the hospital, find a doctor who knows something. Did Vinnie say anything?"

"Not a thing. And he probably won't be saying anything for quite a while. But there was this," Johnson said, pulling a crime scene photograph from his jacket pocket and handing it across the table to me.

"What is it?"

"The floor near Vinnie's body."

The photo was a close-up shot of two symbols written in blood.

X X

"Mean anything to you?"

"It does. Vinnie is telling us he was double-crossed."

2

It was nearly two hours before I was able to talk to a doctor and hear what I didn't want to hear.

It was after three in the morning when I made it back home.

Another fun-filled Saturday night.

I knew exactly where Darlene would be with Tug McGraw five hours later, so I set my alarm for seven-thirty.

It would have given me four hours sleep, had I been able to sleep.

I sat on a bench in Buena Vista Park, waiting for Darlene and the dog to come to the end of their run.

They were about to pass the bench at full speed when Darlene spotted me. She stopped on a dime.

I was afraid the leash would pull Tug McGraw's head off.

"I'm not glad to see you," she said.

"Vinnie was shot last night. He's alive, but not in the clear."

"Have you seen him?"

"He went from surgery to recovery to intensive care, no one will be seeing him until noon at the earliest."

"What happened?"

"The going theory is Vinnie shot a man named Hanover while Vinnie was committing a robbery, but we both know that's not true."

"What's your theory?"

"I think someone else was there, shot them both, and staged the scene to mislead the police."

"Hanover?"

"Dead."

"So, on top of everything, Vinnie is a murder suspect."

"I'm hoping when the crime scene investigators are through they'll find it couldn't have gone down that way."

"What was Vinnie doing there?"

"Before he lost consciousness at the scene, Vinnie left a message. He was telling us he had been betrayed. Someone Vinnie felt he could trust got him there, and back-stabbed him. That someone is who we're looking for."

"What can I do to help find that *someone*?"

"I don't know enough yet to answer that question, but there is something you can do. Ray Boyle called to tell me he put Vinnie's mother on a plane, can you pick her up at the airport and take her to the hospital?"

"Of course. What will you be doing?"

"I'll be paying a polite visit to a nasty Irishman."

3

The Blarney Stone was one of those neighborhood bars where locals came to drink breakfast.

The place was buzzing at nine in the morning.

I went to the bartender and asked for Conway. The barkeep told me to come back later, but didn't say how much later.

"What's your name?" I asked him.

"Paddy."

I might have guessed.

"Paddy, if Big Bill happens to be available sooner than later, please let him know Jake Diamond needs to talk."

Paddy picked up the bar phone, exchanged a few words, and sent me back to Conway's office.

"Jake Diamond. Take a seat. I'm guessing you are here about Vinnie Strings."

"Vinnie was shot last night."

"That's terrible news. Is he alive?"

"Afraid you may not get what he owes you?"

"May I call you Jake?"

"Sure."

"Jake. I was raised by an Irish mother, I'm not heartless. And that was a rude thing to say. I'll let it go this time. I'm sure you are upset."

"I apologize. Vinnie is alive, but it's touch and go. Any idea about who may have wanted to hurt him?"

"None. I saw him yesterday afternoon, and I gave him a one-week grace period to square his debt. I suggested he reach out to you for help. He wasn't too keen on that idea. Vinnie is a luckless gambler, but he has his pride. I am a businessman and I can't tolerate being short-changed, but I actually like the kid. I have many eyes and ears around the city. If I get wind of anything at all, I'll let you know."

"Thank you."

"How about a drink. I have twenty-one-year-old Jameson."

"It's a little early for me."

"It's five in the afternoon in Dublin," Big Bill said.

4

I arrived at Saint Francis Memorial just before eleven.

I found Darlene and Vinnie's mother sitting in the visitors lounge at the intensive care unit.

Frances Stradivarius rose from her seat, moved to me, and took me in her arms. Then she stepped back and looked me in the eyes.

"Tell me my son will be all right."

I told her Vinnie would be all right.

"They won't let me see him."

"I'll try to locate the doctor I spoke with last night, try to find out when you can see Vinnie. And I need coffee. Have you had anything to eat? Can I bring you something from the cafeteria? The food isn't terrible."

"I couldn't eat. Maybe a cup of hot tea."

"Will you be all right if I go with Jake?" Darlene asked. "I'll be back soon."

"Yes, dear, go on."

Darlene and I walked toward the elevator.

"Find out when she can see Vinnie," Darlene said. "Frances will go nuts if she has to wait much longer. I'll go down to the cafeteria for takeout."

Darlene took the stairs down.

I went off to find a doctor.

The good news was that Frances would be able to see her son soon.

The bad news was that Vinnie would not know she was there.

On my way back to the lounge, I got a call from Sergeant Johnson.

He asked about Vinnie, I told him what I knew.

Johnson said he had some information and asked if I could come down to Vallejo Street Station.

I took a seat beside Vinnie's mother.

"You can see Vinnie soon, thirty minutes. But you need to be prepared, Frances. He won't be conscious, and they have a machine hooked up to help him breathe."

"My God. Can I sit by him and hold his hand?"

"Of course," I said. "I need to see someone. Darlene should be back any minute. Will you be okay?"

"I'm trying my best, Jake, go ahead."

I bumped into Darlene at the elevator.

She was carrying a cardboard tray holding three paper cups and three wrapped sandwiches.

She handed me a cup of coffee.

"How's Vinnie?"

"The jury is still out."

"Going somewhere?"

"Vallejo Street. Johnson has something for me."

"Did Big Bill have anything?"

"No. But he did offer to ask around, and offered me an Irish breakfast."

"Corn beef and cabbage?"

"Jameson."

"Take this," she said, handing me one of the sandwiches. "Scrambled egg and cheese on a hard roll."

"No bacon?"

"Give me a break, Jake."

"We'll need to find a hotel for Frances. We can't let her see Vinnie's apartment."

"She can stay at my place. There's plenty of room, and Tug McGraw loves company."

"Thanks."

"If you want to thank me, find the bastard who hurt Vinnie."

"We will," I said, and I stepped into the elevator.

5

Johnson rose from his seat when I reached his desk at the Vallejo Street Police Station.

"Follow me," he said. "Lopez wants in on this."

The door to her office was open. She waved us in.

"Take a seat," she said.

We sat.

Captain Laura Lopez and I had a history of conflict. She often referred to me as a thorn in her side. But I had helped Lopez out of a jam recently, and I knew she had a soft-spot for Vinnie Strings.

"I was truly sorry to hear the news," Lopez said. "Is Vinnie going to pull through?"

I had heard the same question too many times, and had nothing to offer but a different version of the same answer.

"To paraphrase the doctors. *Heads he will, tails he won't.*"

Lopez left it at that.

"Sergeant Johnson received preliminary findings from the forensics unit. I've asked him to fill us both in."

"Investigators have not been able to learn anything about the gun that killed Hanover, other than the fact it was at Vinnie's side and it tested positive for his fingerprints. The gun fired at Vinnie was registered to Hanover. Small traces of gunpowder residue were found on Vinnie's hand, and Hanover's also. It is still being considered a robbery homicide, and we don't expect that to change until when and if Vinnie is able to give us something else to go on."

"There was someone else there," I said.

"That will be a very hard sell. The place was loaded with valuables. The painting on the wall behind Hanover's desk alone was appraised at six figures. Not to mention an impressive coin collection in plain sight in the office, and the twelve hundred dollars in cash found in Hanover's wallet. It doesn't seem as if anything was taken. Hanover's daughter is coming from New York City for the identification and the funeral. We can ask her to look through the house, she may be able to tell us if something is obviously missing."

Lopez finally spoke up.

"Vinnie Stradivarius is a habitual screw up, but I don't believe he could rob someone. Let alone shoot and kill someone. I don't know if or how we can help him, but we will do what we can."

I thanked them both and headed back to the hospital.

6

I found Darlene pacing back and forth in front of Vinnie's hospital room.

"Have you seen him?"

"Not much to see. He looks like he's sleeping peacefully. Of course, all the tubes and monitors and machines plugged into him take something away from the picture of serenity."

"Frances?"

"She's in there holding his hand. What did Johnson have?"

I ran it by her.

"Did you see your dream girl?"

"Lopez expressed her condolences and her interest in helping."

"What a gal. Look, Jake, I really need to get away from here for a while. I dislike hospitals more than I dislike date movies. I told Frances I would come back for her when she's ready to leave, if she'll *ever* be ready to leave. Call my cell if you need anything, I'll be at Ocean Beach keeping a promise to my dog."

Although I didn't mind date movies, as long as Sandra Bullock or Goldie Hawn weren't involved, my dislike of hospitals rivaled Darlene's. In addition to that, I was dog-tired from lack of sleep. And, I wasn't looking forward to seeing Vinnie hooked up to a roomful of contraptions. But I felt I should at least go in and see how Frances was doing, tell her I needed to get some rest, and ask for her permission to leave.

I was pacing in front of the room, as Darlene had earlier, looking foolish trying to decide whether to go in or not go in, when an attractive young woman approached me.

"You're Jake Diamond," she said.

"Is that a question?"

"No, you're Jake Diamond."

"And you are?"

"Rachel Palmer. I wait tables at The Homestead on Fulton. I've seen you there with Vinnie a few times, he talks about you like you're a superstar."

"Vinnie tends to exaggerate. Are you a friend of his?"

"Vinnie comes into the bar occasionally. We've talked. He's a good guy. I heard what happened. I came to see how he was doing."

"Not great," I said. I was running out of colloquialisms. "It's good of you to come."

"It's funny. Well, not funny really. I saw him just yesterday afternoon."

"At The Homestead?"

"Yes. Vinnie was unusually quiet, and knocking down gin and tonics. He seemed preoccupied, like something was worrying him. I don't feel familiar enough with Vinnie to ask about his troubles, so I didn't."

I felt sure Vinnie had Big Bill Conway on his mind.

"Vinnie was alone?"

"At first, but then a friend joined him at the booth."

"A friend?"

"They seemed friendly. I've seen him with Vinnie once or twice before. I think they play cards together."

"Have a name?"

"Bobby."

"Last name?"

"No. Bobby is all I have."

"Vinnie won't be seeing visitors for a while. His mother is in with him now, but she is a different story."

"That's okay. I just wanted to find out what I could. I'm glad Vinnie has family around. I hope he comes through. He's a good guy."

"I'll drop by The Homestead and let you know when he is entertaining guests again."

"That would be good," she said, with a genuine smile.

"And if Bobby comes in again, would you please give me a shout," I said, handing her a business card.

"I will. Good luck."

"With what?"

"Finding whoever did this to your friend."

After Rachel walked off, I quietly opened the door to Vinnie's room and I peeked in. His mother had moved a chair as close as possible to the bed. She sat holding her son's hand in hers, and she was fast asleep.

I just as quietly closed the door, and left to get some shuteye myself.

7

The phone woke me up at six in the evening. Darlene.

"I'm at my house with Frances. Somehow, I finally extracted her from the hospital. Vinnie's doctor said they would call if there was any change."

"Vinnie ever mention a friend named Bobby?"

"Not that I recall, what's that about?"

"I'm not sure. Maybe nothing."

"There's Chinese food on the way here, if you're hungry."

"I'll pass, I had it last night."

"Okay. You know how to reach me."

I was reminded I hadn't taken a bite to eat since the breakfast sandwich, and not a morsel of meat all day.

I decided to go down to Carlucci's Restaurant, hoping I might bump into Tony. Even though seeing Tony Carlucci was not my idea of a good time.

In any case, Mama Carlucci would insist I eat far too much food.

I decided to take a cab—in case it took far too much wine to wash it all down.

I didn't spot Carlucci, but then Tony had a strict policy. He would never interrupt someone while they took their meal.

"Espresso?" the waiter asked, when he was clearing the plates.

"Sure."

He came back with a tray. Two coffees, two small glasses, a bottle of Sambuca, and assorted biscotti.

Only then did Carlucci appear at the table.

"I was sorry to hear about Vinnie. If there is anything I can do to help, don't hesitate."

Everyone was sorry to hear about Vinnie, and everyone wanted to help.

Vinnie was well liked.

I did not like asking Tony Carlucci for help. There always managed to be strings attached. And Tony didn't like to offer, but his big brother Johnny Boy, who called San Quentin home, insisted Tony be nice. A curse and a blessing.

"Maybe you *can* help."

"Shoot."

I hated when Carlucci said shoot.

"How well do you know the regular poker games in town?"

"Looking to buy into one?"

"No. I want to know what games Vinnie might sit in on. I'm looking for someone he plays with."

"Have a name?"

"Bobby."

"That's it?"

"That's it."

"There are lots of games, and a lot of cats named Bobby. If you come up with anything more specific, I'll see what I can do."

"Fair enough. Thanks," I said, finishing the espresso with a taste of the sweet liqueur.

"I'll walk you to your car."

"I came by cab."

"Then I'll give you I ride home. I was leaving anyway."

I didn't really care to have Carlucci know where I lived.

"You don't need to bother."

"No bother at all. I know where you live, it's on my way."

. . .

I knew I would be up for quite a while, having indulged in a four-hour afternoon nap.

I tried mapping out a plan for the next day, but everything I came up with depended on a *maybe*.

Maybe Big Bill Conway knew something about a Bobby.

Maybe Bobby would show up at The Homestead and Rachel would call.

Maybe Johnson or Lopez would learn something new.

Maybe Vinnie would come awake and clear it all up.

I opened the book I was reading and found David Copperfield where I had last left him.

David was visiting the home of the Peggotty family.

They lived in a boat turned upside down.

I could relate.

8

I was up until three, but Charles Dickens and George Dickel had kept me well entertained.

The phone woke me at seven on Monday morning.

Sleeping four hours at a time was a not a habit I was interested in permanently adopting.

I answered on the third ring.

Darlene.

"I dropped Frances off at the hospital. They stopped pumping Vinnie full of antibiotics, it seems the danger of serious infection is past. He hasn't been awake yet, and still needs help breathing. They're still feeding him through a tube."

"Too bad, Tony Carlucci offered to send meatballs over to the hospital."

"You went to see Carlucci?"

"I mainly went out to his restaurant to eat, and bumped into him."

"If you didn't want to bump into Carlucci, you could have gone to Burger King. Was he any help?"

"Anthony was willing but unable. But it was worth a shot, the grub was outstanding. Where are you now?"

"I just walked into the office. I'm about to check the answering machine with the hope there is something there beside another low-interest credit card offer or a three-dollar discount for Great Clips, though you could use a haircut. It's getting dangerously close to the first of the month, we need some business. You know, like when you do a job for someone and they actually pay you."

"Attorneys use private investigators, maybe we should start chasing lawyers who are chasing ambulances."

"That's an idea. Are you planning to make an appearance here?"

"Soon. Can I bring you anything?"

"George Clooney."

After a shower and a shave, I looked and felt much better.

I did need a haircut.

I grabbed a breakfast burrito at Little Chihuahua on my way to see Conway, so I wouldn't be tempted to start my day with Irish whiskey.

I was hoping Big Bill didn't know more than five or six poker players named Bobby.

This time, Paddy at the bar sent me back to Conway's office without the song and dance.

"I know at least five or six card players called Bobby."

Terrific.

"But," Conway added, "I do know Vinnie sat in at a game down at Fort Mason, second and fourth Monday of every month. And today happens to be the fourth Monday."

"Where at Fort Mason?"

"They use a small theater, The Changing Scene. They set the card table up on the stage, makes it feel like they're in a Tennessee Williams play."

"What time?"

"Usually begins at eight."

"Can I get in?"

"Tell the guy at the door that Tom Collins sent you."

"Tom Collins?"

"Trust me."

. . .

I arrived at the office around ten.

Darlene was at her desk doing what she did better than anyone I knew. Trying to determine which bills to pay first. Tug McGraw was under the desk, gnawing on a rawhide bone that looked as if it came out of a Brontosaurus.

"Tom Romano called."

"And?"

"Poor Tom, I feel sorry for him. He said he had more work than he could handle."

"Sad."

"He asked if we would take a few cases off his hands."

"And you said?"

"*Is the Pope Catholic.* Tom said he would send one case over today."

"Did he say what it was?"

"No, but he did say it wasn't the worst one."

"Any word from Johnson or Lopez?"

"No, but doesn't Johnson have your cell number?"

"Battery's dead."

"Ever think of charging your phone overnight?"

"Sometimes. I got a lead from a waitress at The Homestead. She saw Vinnie there Saturday afternoon, with a guy named Bobby."

"Bobby have a last name?"

"Probably."

"Great. Talk about clues."

"I just came from seeing Big Bill again."

"And?"

"I'm going out to Fort Mason tonight. There's a card game Vinnie sat in on regularly, and it seems Bobby played at the same table as Vinnie at times. It could be an entirely different game, but a lead is a lead."

"As they say."

The phone on Darlene's desk rang.

"Diamond Investigations, no job too small. Yes. Yes. Sure.

Thanks. Ciao."

"Let me guess. Romano?"

"Our new client will be here at two."

"Perfect. It will rule out the afternoon nap."

"And give you plenty of time to stuff yourself with fried squid."

"Is that today's lunch special?"

"Yes, Jacob, it's High Cholesterol Monday once again."

9

Darlene and I decided to run over to the hospital, not so much expecting a miraculous recovery as to remind Frances Stradivarius that she needed food once in a while. I left my cell phone at the office to charge.

Before leaving, I called Molinari's Italian Salumeria below the office and asked Angelo Verdi to save me a portion of calamari for later that afternoon.

Vinnie was the same. Frances was glued to the side of his bed.

We dragged her down to the cafeteria for lunch.

A little after one, we returned to headquarters to prepare for the arrival of our prospective client.

I waited in the small back room we call my Private Office.

At precisely two, Darlene rang me on the intercom.

"Your appointment is here, Mr. Diamond."

Very professional.

I hadn't been told if we were expecting a man or a woman.

It was a fifty-fifty shot.

"Please send him in."

"She will be right with you," Darlene said.

I rose from my chair as Darlene ushered our guest through the door.

"Jake Diamond, Josephine Leone," Darlene said, then disappeared.

"Please have a seat. May I call you Josephine?"

"Josie will do."

She took the client's chair and I returned to my place behind the desk.

"So, Josie," I said, always one to initiate a conversation with eloquence. "How may we help you?"

"My son is missing."

"Just to be clear. When you say your son is missing, what exactly do you mean?"

"Tim hasn't been home for two days and nights."

"How old is Tim?"

"Sixteen. Last month."

"Have you been to the police?"

"I have, but they don't appear committed."

"Why do you say that?"

"Tim has disappeared, for a day or so, twice before. The first time, I expected him back from school by four. I returned home from the hospital around eight that night, and he wasn't there."

"The hospital?"

"I'm an administrator at Saint Mary's. I often have to work late. By ten, Tim was still not home and I began to worry. I began calling the homes of his friends, the ones I knew of. Nothing. By midnight I was frantic, so I went to the police. Since Tim was fifteen at the time, all the agencies kicked into gear immediately. Be On The Lookout Bulletin, Amber Alert, checking hospitals and morgues. I stayed home the next day, Tim never made it to school. At three he walked into the house as if it was no big deal. With no explanation."

"Was he punished?"

"I was relieved to have him back. Tim has had a hard time since my husband passed away a year ago. Tim worshipped his father. I let it go."

"The second time?"

"The second time he stayed out all night, I waited nearly all of the next day before reporting him missing. After the first incident, I took his absence less seriously. The authorities went through the entire drill again. Then, Tim came home around midnight. I was asleep. The first time, I couldn't sleep at all. Now Tim is sixteen and, as arbitrary as it sounds, the protocol is not the same. The system reacts with less a sense of urgency. And, just as I had felt less concerned the second time Tim went missing, I think the police are weary of *the mom who cried wolf*. But this is the longest he's been gone."

"But, that's not all of it."

"I don't follow."

"Josie, I don't wish to offend you. Tim has been gone a bit longer than before, but I see no reason why he won't be back. He may even be at home as we speak. And, as you said, both you and the police have been getting used to his absences. I believe something else has you *extra* worried. Something you have not told the police about, something you have not told me about."

Josephine Leone took an envelope from her handbag and passed it to me. It was filled with cash.

"I found this in his room."

"Have you counted it?"

"More than eight thousand dollars. What could it mean?"

"It could mean several things, and probably none are good news. Would you mind if my associate joins us?"

I walked over and opened the door to the outer office.

"Darlene, do you have a minute."

Darlene Roman started with me as a receptionist, but soon proved to be so much more. I refer to her as my associate only because she will not allow me to call her *partner*. Darlene is smart, intuitive, and has helped me solve many puzzles. Not to mention, I would not know how to balance a checkbook or manage an internet search without Darlene's assistance. Many times, I've expressed my wish to have her name added to the opaque glass pane on the office door. And as many times she has warned me against it.

Darlene joined us. I quickly brought her up to speed before giving Josie the bad news and the worse news.

"Unless he hit the lottery, a sixteen-year-old with eight thousand dollars in cash has been doing something illegal and potentially dangerous. If I had to guess, when he goes off for a day or two he is probably doing whatever he does to get the money. In that case, he'll be back with more for the envelope. That is the best case. If he doesn't return, and fairly soon, everything changes. He will no longer be considered a runaway."

"Why is that?" Josie asked.

"Because if your son planned to voluntarily leave home permanently, he would not have left the money behind."

"What should I do?"

"I would go to the police, with the envelope this time."

"If Tim has been breaking the law, I could be ruining his life forever. It would be like turning him in."

I looked to Darlene. I could tell the wheels were turning.

And that she wasn't quite ready to jump in.

"Tim's situation may already be beyond repair," I said. "I've told you what I think you should do, but I won't do it for you. People who come to us for help expect confidentiality. If we knew for certain that Tim was in physical danger, we would be compelled to report this conversation. But we don't know that."

"What if I wait a while longer? Tim may return tonight or tomorrow."

"And then what? You'll give him a good talking to? Once he knows you found the cash, he'll be out the door again. I don't know if we can help you."

"We could take a look through his room, maybe find something that can tell us what he's been up to or where," Darlene said. "If Jake thinks it's a good idea."

It wasn't a bad idea.

And, true to form, Darlene left it up to me.

"We can do that," I said.

When we entered the house, we found it had been turned upside down.

"Do you think Tim did this?" Josie asked.

"I don't. If Tim came back for the money and found it gone, he would have waited here for you and confronted you about it. It was someone else."

Tim's bedroom had seen the worst. Every drawer was on the floor, all their contents scattered throughout the room.

Darlene had wandered off and then she joined us in the bedroom.

"Jake. I checked all the windows, the front and back doors, there is no sign of forced entry. Whoever came in must have had a key."

"Tim's key," I said.

"Now, I'm scared," Josie said.

"Now you have no choice but to get the police involved."

"I found this in the back yard," Darlene said, handing me a pen.

A black plastic ballpoint, inscribed with the words Twin Peaks Hotel.

I called Sergeant Johnson.

"All we can do now is wait, and hope for the best. The police are on their way to the hotel. As soon as Johnson has something, he will let us know and I will let you know. Is there somewhere you can go tonight?"

"Go?"

"There's an evidence team headed here, to collect fingerprints and such. And you don't want to spend the night in the middle of this mess."

"I have a sister."

"Where?"

"Upper Haight. Carl Street near Cole."

"We can drive you over," I said.

We watched Josephine walk into her sister's place.

As we pulled away, Darlene's cell phone rang.

"Vinnie woke up," she said, after taking the call.

"Is he talking?"

"He won't be talking for a while yet. We should get to the hospital, see how Frances is doing. And feed her."

10

After dinner in the hospital cafeteria, Frances went back in to sit with Vinnie.

Darlene went in with her, saying she would be out shortly.

I was sitting in the waiting room, waiting, when Johnson called.

"We found the boy. Tied up in a hotel room. We picked up the guy who was holding him—in the bar next door. They are both being questioned now."

"Is the boy all right?"

"Shook up, but not hurt physically."

"I'll call his mother. Will she be able to see him tonight?"

"It may be a while. She's welcome to come down to Vallejo Street and wait if she would like to."

"I'm sure she will. Thanks."

I called Josephine Leone and told her everything I knew.

Darlene came out of Vinnie's room a few minutes later.

I filled her in.

"Quite a day," she said. "So far."

"So far?"

"Don't you need to be at Fort Mason at eight."

"Thanks for reminding me. What time is it now?"

"Six."

"Not enough time to run home for a nap."

"Well, in that case, let's get a drink."

. . .

We walked over to the White Horse Tavern at Sutter and Mason.

We found an empty booth away from the riot near the bar.

"White wine?" I asked Darlene, when a waitress finally found us.

"Cuervo Gold with a beer chaser."

"What's with that?"

"Like I said, it's been quite a day."

I ordered the same.

The waitress returned in record time.

"Here's to Vinnie Stradivarius," Darlene said, raising her shot glass. "He made it."

We tapped our glasses together, and knocked the shots down.

"And here's to another day without making any money," Darlene said, lifting her beer glass.

"After Johnson called, I spoke to Josie. She said she would be sending us a check, equal to the amount in the envelope she found in her son's room. She had considered simply giving us the cash, but figured it was going to be taken into evidence."

"How much?" Darlene asked.

"Eight thousand dollars, and change."

"That won't hurt. How about another shot? A toast to Josie."

"That wouldn't hurt either."

11

I walked Darlene back to the hospital, where she hoped to get Frances the hell out of there for the night.

I checked my phone when I reached my car and saw I had a message.

I didn't know the number. I usually delete those without listening, but I was still hoping for a haircut discount.

It was Rachel, the waitress from The Homestead. She identified herself and added just two words. Bobby Lockhart.

I drove out to Fort Mason.

There was a sentry at the entrance to The Changing Scene Theatre.

"What can I do for you?"

"Bobby Lockhart," I said, feeling that saying *Tom Collins* would sound foolish.

"Don't know him."

"Tom Collins," I said.

Why not.

"Why didn't you say so, what about Bobby Lockhart?"

"Is he here?"

"What's your interest?"

"I need to talk to him about Vinnie Strings."

"Are you a friend of Vinnie's?"

"Yes. Jake Diamond."

It was beginning to feel like the name game.

"Jake Diamond. I've heard Vinnie speak of you many times. I heard what happened, is he going to make it?"

Finally, I could say yes.

"Yes. How about Lockhart."

"Bobby didn't show up tonight. With both Lockhart and Vinnie out, we're shorthanded."

"Sorry to hear it. Do you know where Lockhart lives?"

"I don't know where anyone lives, I just let them in and out. But I'm sure Conway could have told you, saved you a trip out here."

"I didn't have a last name at the time."

"And Bobby is a common name."

I didn't know what to say to that.

I turned and headed back to my car.

"Tell Big Bill that Slick said hey," he called after me.

12

Bobby Lockhart sat in his apartment alone. Drinking.

The knocking got him to his feet.

Lockhart rushed over and opened his door.

The visitor standing there was holding a small leather satchel.

"Who are you?" Bobby asked.

"Just a messenger, with your delivery."

"The cash?"

"Yes."

"All of it?"

"Fifty thousand dollars. Right?"

"*Damn* right. Christ, I've been waiting two fucking days."

"May I come in?"

"Yes, you can come in."

"It had to wait until today, when the bank opened."

"Well, better late than never. As they say."

"I heard you brought someone with you to Hanover's, and the other man survived."

"Don't worry about him, he's not going to make it."

"You were specifically told to go alone."

"It was supposed to look like an attempted robbery gone bad. The way I left the scene it should be open and shut, even for San Francisco's dumbest."

"I also heard the other man has a clean record, and now he has friends trying to find out what happened."

"Look. I ran into someone I knew. He was handy. Are you going to tell me everything you've heard, or are you going to hand over the money?"

The visitor's eyes scanned the room, finally resting on a small corner table.

"Did you take that from Hanover's house?"

"Take what?"

"The angel."

"What if I did?"

"At the risk of sounding repetitive, weren't you specifically instructed not to remove anything?"

"It caught my eye. I like angels," Lockhart said, turning his attention to the small figure. "Look at how delicate her wings are. Nobody is going to miss the thing."

When Bobby turned back to his visitor, he was facing a .357 Magnum. Pointed at his face.

"What? You're going to kill me for lifting a tiny fucking statue."

"No, Bobby. I was going to kill you anyway."

NOTHING IS NOTHING

The only two things you can truly depend upon
are gravity and greed.
—Jack Palance

13

I left Fort Mason and drove out to the Blarney Stone for the third time in two days, having never taken a drink there.

I was hoping Big Bill could help me locate Bobby Lockhart.

If not, I could at least give him Slick's regards.

I found him at the bar this time, and let him talk me into a twenty-one-year-old Jameson.

"It always helps to be specific.," Conway said, when I was able to give him a full name. "Bobby has always been a bad seed. In and out of trouble throughout his teens. Bobby had a crush on Pamela Miller in high school. Beautiful girl, she looked like Lana Turner. Future Prom Queen. Of course, Pamela was dating the varsity football quarterback. Eric Campbell. Bobby broke Eric's leg in three places. A real tragedy. Campbell never played again, and the kid could throw a football like Joe Montana. Lockhart dropped out of school, joined the Marines, and was sent to Kuwait during Desert Shield. It took him six months to earn a Dishonorable Discharge. Bobby has been in and out of jails since then. I knew Bobby's old man. Frankie Lockhart was a mean son-of-a-bitch. At San Quentin, Frankie nearly killed another inmate with a plastic spoon. He shoved it so far up into the poor bastard's ear, only about a sixteenth of an inch showed. Just enough for them to grab it and yank it out with needle nose pliers."

At another time, I might have found the Lockhart family history colorful.

"Do you know where I can find Bobby Lockhart?" I asked, trying not to appear impolite.

"I do, if he's at home."

"Could you give me an address?"

"Why don't we go over together. Bobby doesn't take to strangers. Drink up. I'll have my driver bring the car around front."

When Conway's driver pulled up to Lockhart's apartment building, the place was crawling with cops.

A police officer walked up to the car.

The uniform was asking the driver to move the vehicle, when Detective Lance Wright appeared.

"I've got this, Jimmy," he said, and the uniform moved off.

Conway powered down the back window of the Town Car.

"Big Bill," Wright said, "what brings you out here?"

"I was hoping to have a chat with Bobby Lockhart."

"You're too late."

"Dead?"

"Dead as Lincoln."

"Well I guess that's that. Have a good night, Lance."

"I seriously doubt it, Bill."

"What was your interest in Bobby?" Conway asked, when we were heading back to the Barney Stone.

"I had some questions. He may have been the last person to see Vinnie before the shooting."

"I'm sorry you didn't get a chance to talk to him. How is Vinnie doing by the way?"

"Seems like he's out of the woods, but he's not able to speak yet."

"I'm glad to hear he's going to make it."

"About the money Vinnie owes you, I'll take care of it."

"Forget it. Tell him we're square. He deserves a break. But make sure no one else hears about it."

Conway's driver let me out at my car.

"Thanks for your help," I said to Big Bill.

"I wasn't much help in the end, and I think we've seen enough of each other for a while."

14

I had finally made it home, when Johnson called.

"The man who was holding Tim Leone was a loser named Ned Cullum. Tim was collecting numbers money for Cullum, and the kid was skimming off the top. Ned isn't the sharpest knife in the drawer but he eventually figured out, over time, that he was eight thousand light. Ned confronted Tim. Tim played dumb. Cullum took the kid's keys, tied Tim up in the hotel room, and went to the house. When Cullum came back empty-handed, he threatened to kill Tim if the kid didn't produce the cash. The kid was lucky. Cullum went down for a drink first, to give Tim a little time to think it over."

"What happens to Tim?"

"We'll lock him up at juvie hall for a few weeks. Put a good scare into him, and hope it sticks. Not much more we can do. Most of it is going to be about a boy's relationship with his mother. As it often is."

The phone woke me at seven the next morning. Darlene.

"I'm at the hospital, you need to get over here. Now. I need help getting Frances calmed down."

"What's up?"

"Vinnie is able to speak, and they won't let her into his room. They have strict orders, no one talks with Vinnie before the police.

And there is no telling when they will show up. Frances is out of control."

"I'll be right down."

I was out of the house and into my car in ten minutes.

I called Sergeant Johnson on my way to Saint Francis Memorial.

Darlene and I were both working on Frances when Johnson arrived.

"If she doesn't get in to see Vinnie soon, she is going to burn the place down. And if *other* detectives show up to talk to him, they won't let *me* go in with them," I said to Johnson.

"And I would?"

"Would you?"

Johnson walked over to Vinnie's mother.

He sat at her side, and spoke softly.

"Mrs. Stradivarius."

"Yes."

"May I call you Frances?"

"Yes."

"I'm Detective Johnson. I need a little time with Vinnie. Then I will see to it personally that you get to see your son immediately. I'm asking you for a little patience, Frances, and I would like you to relax."

The transformation was dramatic.

Frances never looked so calm.

"Thank you," she said.

"You are very welcome."

Johnson walked to Vinnie's hospital room door, and turned to me.

"Are you coming, or what?"

We walked up to the bed. Vinnie opened his eyes.

"Good to have you back," I said.

"I screwed up again, Jake."

"I'll scold you some other time, Vinnie. For now, try to tell us what happened so we can get your mom in here. She's very anxious."

Vinnie told us what happened on Saturday night.

"I tried to be as still as possible, I didn't breathe. When I heard Bobby leave, I managed to scratch the two letters on the floor. That's all I remember until I woke up here. You need to find Bobby Lockhart."

"We will," Johnson said.

"We'll send your mom in," I said. "I'll be back to see you later."

Frances was standing outside the door like she was at the front of the line for the latest iPhone. She rushed past us without a word.

Johnson and I joined Darlene in the visitor's lounge.

We sat, and I gave Darlene the short version.

"You didn't tell Vinnie that Lockhart was dead," I said to Johnson.

"He has enough worries."

"Did you believe him?"

"I did. But to the district attorney, it's just his word. They have found nothing concrete to show that Lockhart was there."

"Was anything found in Lockhart's apartment? Like a Picasso or a seventeen-ninety-four Flowing Hair Dollar?"

"No. And even if it could be proved that someone else was with Vinnie and Hanover in that room, it would not clear Vinnie for the shooting. I hate saying it. Unless something new turns up, and soon, Vinnie will be charged with murder."

"Johnson tells it like it is." Darlene said, after the sergeant took off.

"Sugar-coating is definitely not his style."

"What now?"

"I have no idea. I do know I need to get out of here. Smell the roses, and get something to eat. Interested?"

"I want to see Vinnie before I leave. Then I should get down to the office and start paying bills, with the hope Josephine Leone's check arrives in time to cover them. By the way?"

"Yes?"

"Is a seventeen-ninety-four Flowing Hair Dollar extremely valuable?"

"I have no idea."

I left, hoping I could find some roses to smell.

15

When I arrived at the office a few hours later, Darlene was sitting at her desk handling the checkbook as if it had teeth.

She didn't appear to be in a good mood.

"I've been trying to reach you. Did you fail to charge your phone again?"

"I turned it off. No news is good news."

"Jennifer Hanover called. She said she would like to speak to you, about her father. I took a chance and told her she could find you here at two. Before you ask me what time it is now, try the clock on the wall."

Darlene was definitely not in a good mood.

I checked the clock. One-forty-five.

"Doesn't give me much time."

"Much time for what?"

I decided on a new approach.

"Where's the pooch?"

"I sent him off to visit my friend and her kids at Stinson Beach. I asked them to call when McGraw was done with the dinosaur bone. Oh, and Angelo called from the delicatessen downstairs. Wants to know how long you would like him to hold the calamari."

"Let me know when Hanover's daughter arrives."

"Good idea."

I gave up and headed for my back office.

"Jake."

"Yes?"

"I'm fooling with you. Granted, I'm in a foul mood. What with Vinnie's situation and our debts and how loud Frances snores when she sleeps. You have to admit, there is not a lot to be festive about. I *will* let you know when she arrives, and you do have enough time to change your shirt and find a tie."

"Good idea."

Darlene led Jennifer Hanover into the back office.

"Will you be needing me here, sir?" Darlene said.

I nearly laughed.

"I'll buzz you if I do."

Darlene left.

"Please, take a seat," I said. "May I call you Jennifer?"

"Jenny is good."

We both sat.

"How can I help you?"

"I understand the man who shot my father is a good friend of yours, and you don't believe he is guilty."

"I know he is *not* guilty."

"You believe someone else was responsible?"

"I do. I believe there was someone else there. Someone who did all of the shooting and tried to make it look otherwise."

"Any idea who?"

"I had a suspect, but he's not talking. Ever."

"Why are the police discounting the possibility?"

"Because there appeared to be nothing of great value removed, and no evidence found to indicate someone else was present. And because the police don't deal in possibilities."

"Yet, you feel convinced."

"Yes."

"The police asked me to go through the house, to see if I noticed anything missing. I was accompanied by two officers.

They won't let anyone look around unescorted until the house is no longer a crime scene. I am fairly familiar with my father's most valuable assets. Paintings, coins, and stamps. But since his collections changed regularly, I can't be absolutely sure of what I should expect to find there. My father may have sold valuables over the years, may even have given some away as gifts."

"Not much help there."

"If your friend did kill my father, I hope he pays for it. If it was someone else, I need to know and see justice done. And I would not want your friend punished for a crime he did not commit. If you believe you can prove someone else was responsible, I would like to hire you to try."

"I'm not exactly sure where to start now, with my prime suspect gone, but we intend to do everything we can to see that our friend is not labeled a murderer. No one needs to hire us for that."

"I understand. Is there anything else I can tell you that might help?"

"Not that I can think of at the moment. Can you think of anything?"

"Not at the moment."

"How long will you be in town?"

"As long as I need to be. I have my father's affairs to attend to, as soon as I can get back into the house. I took an extended leave from my job."

"How can I reach you?"

"I'm staying at the Hotel Griffon on Steuart Street."

I knew the place. The Griffon sat on the San Francisco Bay along the Embarcadero waterfront, with views of the Bay Bridge.

"What do you do for work in New York City?"

"I'll bore you with that some other time. Now, I need to get over to the funeral home. The service and burial are tomorrow morning."

. . .

"Well?" Darlene asked, after Jennifer Hanover left.

"She wanted to hire us to find out who killed her father, if Vinnie didn't."

"And you said something like *we don't need to be paid for that.*"

"Yes."

"You are a good man, Jake."

"I wish I was good and smart."

"I'm off to see Vinnie, pick up Frances, and take her to the supermarket. She's cooking dinner tonight, and would like you to join us. Maybe something Ukrainian. Did you know she was half Ukrainian?"

"I did. And half Cuban."

"No kidding. I should get her together with my father. They might have a lot in common."

"I doubt it."

"My father is Cuban, and his grandfather was Russian."

"Nicolai is mellow. Frances is skittish."

"Good word."

"Vinnie's dad had a handful with Frances, but they adored each other. Sarge Stradivarius was the classic rambling, gambling man. He would have looked right at home on a Mississippi riverboat in the eighteen-fifties, or in a saloon in Dodge City. His father's people came from Poland, and his mother's people from Ireland."

"That makes Vinnie a Cuban-Ukrainian-Polish-Irishman."

"Vinnie is only Vinnie," I said. "What time is dinner?"

"Seven."

"Should I bring vodka or rum?"

16

Frances cooked Cuban.

Darlene did invite her father.

I brought both vodka *and* rum.

And Tempranillo wine, and fruit. For sangria.

The food was spectacular, despite the fact there was not a trace of meat.

Lentil picadillo. Fresh homemade tortillas. Spinach croquetas. Ensalada Cubana. Moros y cristianos.

After Café Bustelo espresso and homemade flan, Frances, Darlene and Nicolai tried teaching me Cuban Canasta. I picked up the basics well enough to get through a hand, but not well enough to be anyone's favorite partner.

I took comfort in knowing I could annihilate any of them at pinochle.

Nicolai and Frances got along very well, in spite of their very different temperaments. I couldn't imagine any romance in the cards, but I could see the makings of a friendship.

They shared dramatic stories, told to Nicolai by his father and Frances by her mother, of life in Cuba before the fall of Batista and after the rise of Castro.

It was late, and Frances was planning to be back at the hospital at the crack of dawn.

Darlene's father didn't drive, he had come over by streetcar, so I offered to give Nicolai a ride home.

"I would like to thank you," Nicolai said, as we drove to his house.

"All I did was cut up some fruit and drop it into a pitcher of wine."

"And managed to procure a bottle of Havana Club Seleccion de Maestros, which is an achievement."

It was Nicolai Roman's polite way of saying illegal. With Tony Carlucci in a helping mood, it wasn't that difficult to *procure.*

"I'm glad you enjoyed it."

"I did very much, but that is not it. I know your work can at times be dangerous. I wish to thank you for protecting my daughter from danger."

"It is my greatest concern."

"I was pleased to hear that Vincent is going to be all right, physically, but Darlene tells me he is facing serious trouble."

"Possibly."

"My daughter is very fond of him."

"My friend and mentor, Jimmy Pigeon, became a second father to Vinnie after Vinnie's father died. When Jimmy died, I sort of inherited Vinnie. Not so much as another father as a regularly frustrated bigger brother. But, with the exception of Frances, there is no one who cares more deeply about Vinnie, or has done more for him, than Darlene. Your daughter has a large heart."

"Darlene makes me very proud. Jake, are you opposed to talking shop?"

"No."

"Darlene explained Vincent's situation in great detail, while Frances was preparing the wonderful meal. Would you mind if I think out loud?"

"Please do."

"Darlene believes Vincent's account without reservation. And since she does, I do. Vincent said he accompanied another man to the house of the man who was killed."

"Bobby Lockhart. And the victim was Frederick Hanover."

"I am basing my observations on Vincent's account. As related to me by Darlene, as related to her by you. If anything germane seems to have been lost in translation, please let me know."

"I will."

"Lockhart asked Vinnie to go with him to Hanover's home for the purpose of collecting a debt. Vinnie was offered compensation and he was led to believe there was nothing nefarious involved. When Hanover greeted them at the door, Vincent felt what Darlene described to me as *uncertainty*."

"Vinnie told me and Detective Johnson he felt, for reasons he could not clearly explain, that Hanover did not recognize Bobby Lockhart at the door."

"Detective Johnson, is he a friend?"

"Something like that."

"Did he believe Vinnie's account?"

"Yes."

"Then, he is a very good ally to have. Jake, I may be expressing thoughts you have already considered, and if so please let me know. And please take no offense, I have the highest regard for your intuitive skills."

"None taken, Nicolai. My concern for Vinnie's survival may have possibly dulled my analytical thinking."

"Or, perhaps, your concern has had you *overthinking*."

"I've been known to do that."

"Let us assume Hanover did not know Bobby Lockhart. In that case, the reason Lockhart gave to Vinnie for the visit, the collection of a debt, would have been false. And, if collecting a debt was not the purpose of Lockhart's visit, one wonders what Lockhart's true purpose was."

"Go on."

"If Lockhart was there to rob Hanover there were, as I understand, many valuable items on hand. Many worth hundreds of thousands of dollars. Yet it appears he took nothing. If he was not there to rob Hanover, he may have had a much more sinister motive. I am suggesting that if Lockhart did not go there to rob Hanover, then he went there to kill Hanover. I hope, that in expressing my thoughts, I have not been out-of-line."

"I think you may be right on track. But if your assessment is correct, it may not help Vinnie's cause."

"How is that?"

"The motive for robbery is fairly clear. Someone wants something that belongs to someone else. A motive for murder is far more difficult to uncover, and prosecutors tend to choose the most reliable path to a conviction. If they do not subscribe to the hypothesis of a premeditated murder, which they'll be disinclined to do unless given strong proof of motive, it would be a lot simpler to make a case for homicide during the commission of a robbery. And that is what Vinnie will be charged with, unless there is contradictory evidence. More than that, even if we can discover undisputed proof that Lockhart had murder in mind from the start, a jury would need to be convinced that Vinnie was not aware of Lockhart's intention."

"Then you must find such evidence and such proof."

"That is easier said than done, Nicolai."

"Most things are easier said than done, Jake. But trying to discover the truth is the noblest of pursuits."

17

I met Darlene at the hospital early the next morning.

"How is Vinnie?"

"The good news is that he is doing much better. The bad news is that he is feeling well enough to wish his mother was not hovering over his bed all day, and lucid enough to understand he will likely be charged with murder."

"Did you give him that idea?"

"No, Jake. I try to be more positive. Vinnie is a simple man, but he is not an idiot."

"Your father is a very wise man."

"He has had very good reason to be. What brought that up? Surely not simply a comparison between Nicolai Roman and Vinnie Strings."

I summarized Nicolai's insights.

"I'm hungry. I'm going down to the cafeteria to see if I can actually find something I can eat."

"Is that all you have to say?"

"Oh, wait. I almost forgot. I know why Bobby Lockhart wanted to kill Frederick Hanover. How's that?"

"Give me a minute. I want to talk to Vinnie alone, maybe I can sweet talk Frances into joining you."

I tapped on the door a few times before walking in.

"Good morning, Frances. Good morning, Vin."

"Jake, thanks for dropping by," Vinnie said.

"It was on my way to the gym."

"Since when do you go to a gym?"

"Just kidding with you, buddy. Frances?"

"Yes."

"Darlene is going down to the cafeteria to look for something she can eat. Like organic yogurt. Since there is no chance she will find any, I was thinking you could go with her. To give her moral support."

"And you want to talk to Vincent alone."

"That too."

Frances gave Vinnie's hand a squeeze, and left the room.

"I have a question, Vin."

"Shoot."

"You told us you had a feeling Hanover didn't know who Bobby was. Could you be more specific?"

"It was Hanover's reaction when he came to the door. It almost stopped me from going in. And then when Hanover offered up the cash in his wallet, I was more confused."

"If Hanover owed Bobby fifteen thousand dollars, for whatever reason, Hanover would surely have known Lockhart."

"The thought went through my mind, but then everything happened so fast. What are you driving at, Jake?"

"I think Bobby's intention, all along, was to kill Hanover."

"That could make me an accomplice to murder."

"You're innocent, and you were a victim. All we need to do is prove it."

"Simple as that?"

"I'll see to it. You have my word," I said, as a nurse came into the room.

"I need some time with my patient," she said.

I turned back as I walked out of the room.

"I will see to it, Vinnie."

I sat and waited for Darlene and Frances to return.

When they came off the elevator, I stood up and met them halfway.

Frances hurried past me, making a bee line for Vinnie's room.

"Frances told me she wants to move over to Vinnie's place tonight. She wants to get it ready for when Vinnie can come home," Darlene said.

"Getting Vinnie's apartment in condition for human habitation will be challenging. We may need to rent her a Shop-Vac."

"If anyone can do it, Frances can. And don't worry, Jake, I won't be lonesome when she leaves. McGraw returns from his sojourn at the beach tomorrow."

I informed Darlene that I was heading over to the Vallejo Street Police Station.

"Missing Laura Lopez?"

"What's your problem with the lieutenant?"

"She treats you like the plague."

"Actually, she's warmed up some since the time I helped clear her as a murder suspect."

"How warm is she? Has she given you an expensive bottle of single-malt scotch, or a free ticket to the Policeman's Ball?"

"Point taken."

"Jake."

"Yes?"

"You know I only give you a hard time because I like you so much."

"I like you too, Darlene."

"And, Jake," she said, as I stepped into the elevator.

"Yes?"

"Guess what I found down in the cafeteria for breakfast?"

"Organic yogurt."

"Bingo."

18

"Diamond, slow down. Better yet, just keep quiet and let *me* talk for a while. Can you do that?"

"Yes."

"Without interrupting?"

"I'll try my best."

I gave Johnson the floor.

"Nothing has been identified as missing from Hanover's home. Nothing puts Bobby Lockhart in the house, except Vinnie's account."

"Which you said you believed."

"It doesn't much matter what *I* believe."

"It matters to me."

"I thought you were going to be quiet."

"Sorry."

"If Bobby Lockhart *was* there, there is nothing to explain why he would have walked out empty-handed. Nothing has been discovered to connect him to the victim, to suggest Lockhart had a reason to want Hanover dead. And there is nothing to prove Bobby Lockhart's untimely death was anything more than coincidental. Anything is possible. But no matter how Nicolai Roman or you or even I may imagine what went down, nothing is still nothing. All of the evidence, circumstantial or otherwise, points to Vinnie. As a lone perpetrator. And a killer."

"You can't believe Lockhart's murder was coincidental."

"I don't, but that's because I believe Vinnie's story. Those who may not accept his account, like the District Attorney or the police brass—those whose opinion counts—will look at Lockhart's record. Bobby wasn't exactly a model citizen—he could have collected a number of enemies."

"You make it sound hopeless."

"It's certainly not good, but not without hope. We've been questioning Lockhart's motive. What if the simple answer is greed?"

"I'm not sure I follow."

"If Lockhart had no *personal* reason to kill Frederick Hanover, he may have been paid to do so. I think you need to be looking for someone who will benefit from Hanover's death."

"I can't believe I didn't see it."

"Don't beat yourself up, I've been doing this for a very long time. You know what's funny."

"I can't imagine."

"A bad choice of words. Ironic. Frederick Hanover's autopsy showed advanced pancreatic cancer. The coroner said he would not have survived more than several months."

"So, whoever might have wanted Hanover dead only needed to wait a while."

"So, it appears."

"Can you help us try identifying suspects?"

"Some. But I'm a police detective. I can't be going around, without sanction, asking citizens who *they* think may have wanted Hanover dead. Everyone from my captain, to the commissioner, to the mayor, would go ballistic. That's why there are private investigators."

"I wondered about that."

"There *is* something else. We've been contacted by McDonough Fine Art Appraisal. They do work for insurance companies. Just a week ago, they did a comprehensive inventory of everything in Hanover's home valued at more than five grand. They will be coming tomorrow to check everything in the house against their list. If anything is unaccounted for, it may at least support Vinnie's claim that someone else was present Saturday. It may be something, or just more of nothing."

Lieutenant Lopez walked up to Johnson's desk.

"I hate to be the bearer of worse news. I was hoping to dump it into Sergeant Johnson's lap." Lopez said. "I wasn't expecting to find you here, Diamond."

"Go ahead," I said.

"The District Attorney's Office has just drawn up charges against Vincent Stradivarius. Felony murder. He will be arraigned as soon as his caregivers at Saint Francis Memorial Hospital say he is ready. If you think you can find any reason to prevent an indictment, I recommend you find it fast."

When I walked into the office, Darlene was singing *Beautiful Day* aloud.

Doing a fair impression of Bono.

"Jake. It's a fabulous late September morning. Autumn has come to San Francisco, at least in some neighborhoods. The hills are alive with the sound of music."

"What got into you?"

"Frances moves into Vinnie's place this evening, my trusty companion returns tomorrow afternoon, I have the house to myself tonight with what's left of the sangria, and this," she said, holding up a check, "from Josephine Leone. Eight thousand one hundred twenty-two dollars, and not a moment too soon. We are going to make it another month. If we don't eat out too often, and you cut back on the Camel straights. What's new at the jailhouse?"

"We decided someone wanted Hanover dead, badly enough to hire a lame brain like Bobby Lockhart to do the deed."

"I wonder who that could be. I guess we start asking around."

"Where would we begin."

"We begin with Hanover's obituary—it was printed in

Monday's *Chronicle*. I saved it for just this occasion. It's resting on the love seat in your executive office. It's very impressive, complete with names of those he was *survived by*. Family, friends, colleagues. You could start with the daughter, since you have already begun to develop a rapport. Yell if you need any help. Meanwhile, I'm going to disperse this windfall as quickly as possible."

"Has anyone ever told you that you are a laugh a minute, Darlene?"

"I hear it every sixty seconds, Jake."

I sat on the small sofa and picked up the newspaper.

Frederick Hanover's obituary, including a comprehensive biography and a good-sized photograph, covered nearly a half page.

Hanover had come from humble beginnings. His father was a janitor and his mother a seamstress. Frederick was an only child.

He began working at various jobs from the time he was twelve years old. Hanover excelled in high school, and earned a full college scholarship.

He received a master's degree in business administration from Stanford.

At twenty-five, Hanover began purchasing properties that would increase in value exponentially. And began purchasing art.

At the time of his death, Frederick Hanover had one of the finest private art collections in the city.

At forty, he teamed up with an old Stanford schoolmate, Jefferson Talbot, and the two built an empire.

Talbot and Hanover were key developers in a number of major projects from the Mosconi Center to the Giants' ballpark.

Hanover's bio could have served as a dictionary definition of success.

Reading it had me imagining, if only for a moment, what my obituary might look like.

Jacob Diamond, failed actor and marginally successful

private investigator, found at a North Beach restaurant with his head lying in a plate of linguini with red clam sauce.

Hanover was sixty-seven years old.

His wife, Angela Bell Hanover, had passed away twelve years earlier.

He was survived by a son, Richard, thirty-four, and a daughter, Jennifer, thirty-two.

Memorial and burial services were scheduled to take place at Mission Dolores Cemetery on Wednesday morning.

I went back to the front office. Darlene was happily writing checks.

"I think your suggestion that I speak with Jennifer Hanover is a good one. Do you think today is too soon?" I asked.

"Too soon?"

"She buried her father this morning."

"You could call, tell her you're sorry you had to miss the funeral and ask her if it's too soon or not too soon."

"The obituary mentioned a son. Jennifer didn't tell me she had an older brother."

"Did you ask her?"

"No."

The phone on Darlene's desk rang.

"Hold that thought," she said.

After a short conversation, she gave me the latest.

"Doctors expect Vinnie will able to leave his bed, and get around in a wheelchair, by late tomorrow or early Friday."

"Let's hope it's *late* Friday."

"Why?"

"If it's late enough, they'll hold the arraignment until Monday morning."

I told her what Lopez said about the criminal charges against Vinnie.

"Why didn't you tell me as soon as you walked in?"

"You were singing the U2 song, I didn't want to rain on

your parade."

"Did Lopez offer any advice."

"About what?"

"Finding evidence that could clear Vinnie."

"The lieutenant's advice was *hurry*."

19

I left a message for Jennifer Hanover at the Hotel Griffon, asking that she call me at her convenience. Effectively throwing the question of *too soon or not too soon* into her court.

If breakfast is the most important meal of the day, I had missed my shot.

Lunch would have to do.

"Did you stop into Molinari's on your way in?" I asked Darlene.

"I did. If I had a rough estimate of when you might show up, I would have grabbed you a coffee and doughnut."

"Any idea what the lunch special is today?"

"If it's Wednesday, it must be sausage and peppers."

Perfect.

"Jake," Angelo Verdi said, when I walked into the salumeria, "have you been avoiding us?"

"Not at all. It's been a busy week, what with Vinnie and all. I'm sorry I never got in for the calamari."

"No problem. How is Vinnie?"

"Much better. He should be able to get around by tomorrow or Friday. And he is finally able to eat solid food."

"Wonderful. The next time you or Darlene plan to visit the hospital, please let me know and I will fix something special for him."

"He would love it."

"I have sausage and peppers today."

"I heard. Sounds perfect."

"Would you like a plate with a side of pasta or a sandwich?"

Angelo's hot sandwiches on seeded Italian bread were legendary.

I grew up in Brooklyn. Since moving west, I had heard such sandwiches referred to a number of ways. Grinder. Hoagie. Sub. Foot-long. But, for me, there was only one way to describe what Angelo did with sausage and peppers or meatballs or veal parmigiana or potatoes and eggs piled onto a half-loaf of warm bread.

"I'll have the hero, Angelo."

"Jake, I'm worried about my brother and his family," Verdi said, as he was assembling the masterpiece.

"What's happened?"

"It's what might happen."

"What might happen?"

"They could lose their home."

It was, in fact, a beautiful day.

I decided to take my hero to the park.

I found a bench and unwrapped the sandwich, trying to ignore the greedy stares.

I took a man-sized bite before calling Darlene.

"I'm at Union Square. I thought you would prefer I not bring the sausage up to the office."

"I appreciate the consideration."

"Can you do me a favor?"

"Sure."

"Find out all you can about Bayshore Heights Village low-income housing in Daly City."

"Got it. How is the grub?"

"Spectacular."

"Be careful you don't get mugged."

I was two-thirds through the sandwich, fearing that one more nibble would put me to sleep, when a visibly homeless man in a New York Yankees ball cap stopped in front of the bench and looked at me with eyes as wide as the Mississippi River.

As much as I dislike the Yankees, I handed him what remained of the meal. Along with an ample amount of paper napkins.

When I returned to the office, Darlene was preparing to leave.

"I need to pick up some welcome home treats for McGraw, and then I'm heading to the hospital. The information you are after is up on the computer monitor. Where did the tip come from?"

"Tip?"

"Bayshore Heights is all about Talbot and Hanover. Tell me later."

And she was gone.

I sat at her desk and read up on Bayshore Heights Village.

Early in his career, Frederick Hanover had purchased land in Daly City. Less than eight miles south of downtown San Francisco, near the Cow Palace which was home to the annual Grand National Rodeo.

Hanover leased the land to San Mateo County for one-dollar a year for thirty years and donated funds of his own for the development of a housing project, Bayshore Heights Village, which provided affordable homes for two hundred and forty families in one of the most expensive real estate markets in the country.

Hanover had been granted the Community Leadership Award for his contributions.

When Hanover partnered with Jefferson Talbot, all of their

individual real estate holdings would likely have become joint assets.

The thirty-year lease was due to run out in a few months.

Which was what was worrying Angelo Verdi. His brother, Salvatore, lived in a home at Bayshore Heights Village with his wife and two teenage sons.

The Bayshore Heights property value was monumental.

If the lease was not extended, and the land instead made available for the development of private enterprise, for luxury condominiums and high-end retail, Sal Verdi and his family would not be able to afford a comparable living situation anywhere else in the Bay Area.

Along with more than two hundred other families.

I had asked Angelo if he or his brother had any reason to believe the lease would not be extended.

"Not really."

"But?"

"Not to sound cynical. But when there is that kind of money involved, it's reason enough," Angelo said.

I was going through all of the implications of what I had read, when the telephone rang.

Jennifer Hanover.

"I'm available this evening, if you would still like to meet."

"Sure."

"How about I buy you dinner?"

"That's not necessary, I could see you after dinner."

"You would be doing me a favor. I dislike eating alone."

"Sure. Where and when?"

"The concierge at my hotel recommended Quince. Do you know it?"

I did.

The restaurant gave the term *ridiculously expensive* new meaning.

"I do."

"Seven."

"I'll see you then."

Darlene walked into the office soon after.

"Vinnie?"

"He was all excited about getting to cruise in a wheelchair tomorrow until I told him to claim he couldn't handle it until no sooner than late Friday."

"Did he ask why?"

"When I say *trust me, Vinnie,* he never asks why."

"Frances?"

"She's going to Vinnie's crib when she finally leaves the hospital today, said she will see me tomorrow."

"Did you stock up goodies for Tug McGraw?"

"You bet I did. Fresh organic dog food, a rawhide bone the size of Rhode Island, and assorted treats for when he's a good boy."

"What constitutes good behavior?"

"When I take him for his morning walk and he poops in less than fifteen minutes. What are your plans for dinner?"

"Jennifer Hanover is treating me to dinner. At Quince."

"Quince. There's not even an appetizer on the menu priced less than thirty dollars."

"I know. I checked the menu after she called."

"Did you take a look at the wine list? They have bottles priced as high as eleven-hundred bucks. Makes one wonder what kind of work she does in New York City to make ends meet."

"She insisted. She said she doesn't like having dinner alone."

"Too bad she won't dine with less than two other people. What did you think about the Bayshore Heights story? And where *did* you get the tip?"

I told her about Angelo Verdi's concerns.

"It sounds as if Frederick Hanover may have been standing in the way of a big business opportunity. You may want to casually bring it up over dinner, and remember to ask why she failed to mention big brother. I am going to call it a day, get home and enjoy the solitude. And, Jake."

"Yes?"

"Do you own a decent suit?"

"I have a very expensive suit. A gift from Johnny Boy Carlucci. I've never had the occasion to wear it. I thought I would save it to be buried in."

"Wear it tonight. I'll make sure to get it cleaned for your funeral. And one more thing."

"Yes?"

"If you can't finish the meal, take the rest with you. They probably use sterling silver boxes for leftovers."

20

I won't try to describe the meal, since much of it I couldn't pronounce.

The food, presentation and service were top-notch—but if push came to shove, I would probably go with Angelo's sausage and peppers hero.

I'm a man of simple tastes.

And, considering the surroundings, I decided that asking for a doggy bag would be inappropriate.

We did talk. I decided against beating around the bush.

"Jenny, please believe I don't wish to alarm you unnecessarily."

"I'm sure you don't. I've had an alarming week already. I can't imagine what could surprise me at this point."

"The man we believe killed your father was Bobby Lockhart. Lockhart told my friend, Vinnie, they were going to pick up a debt your father owed to Lockhart. That was untrue. We also believe Lockhart did not go to the house to rob your father."

"Why then? And who is the *we* you are referring to?"

"Several colleagues have helped me think this through. And we agree that Lockhart went to your father's home for one purpose only. To kill him."

She looked at me as if I had just informed her that her hair was on fire.

"What reason would he have to kill my father?" she finally

asked.

"None."

"You lost me."

"We don't believe Lockhart knew your father at all, he likely never saw your father until that night. We believe Lockhart was a hired gun. The fact that Lockhart was killed two days later supports that conclusion."

"You are saying someone paid the man to murder my father."

"That's what we believe."

"There it is."

"There what is?"

"The surprise I couldn't imagine. And here is where you ask me if there is anyone I can think of who may have wanted my father dead."

"I realize it's a horrible thing to consider. But, yes. Can you think of anyone who might benefit from his death?"

"Would you do me a favor?" she asked, reaching into her purse.

"Of course."

She removed a credit card and passed it to me.

"Would you please take care of the bill. I need some air, and a few minutes to allow all of this to sink in. I'll meet you out front."

We walked along the Embarcadero toward her hotel.

"Do you mind if we sit for a while?" she asked, her first words since leaving the restaurant.

"Not at all."

We settled on a bench, looking out at the bridge and the lights of Oakland reflecting on the bay.

"In spite of the fact that the outcome would have been the same, it would be easier for me to accept that my father was trag- ically killed in a robbery gone bad rather than to imagine he was targeted for assassination. My father was a gentle and generous man. He was well liked and respected, and he had no enemies I am aware of.

"You asked who might benefit from my father's death. I immediately thought of Jefferson Talbot. I've seen the movies and read the mystery novels. When considering murder suspects, the spouse and the business partner are often at the top of the list. I don't know for certain about what happens with the business now, it will depend on what arrangements were agreed upon by both partners. I imagine either the company goes entirely to the survivor or my father's share goes to a designated beneficiary. If my father's death makes Talbot sole owner, one *could* say Talbot will benefit. But Talbot and my father were partners for more than twenty-five years and were extremely successful as a *team*. I can't see a motive there."

"What do you know about Bayshore Heights Village?"

"I know it was one of my father's proudest achievements."

"Were you aware that the lease for the land, presently held by San Mateo County, runs out in a few months?"

"I wasn't."

"Do you believe your father would have wanted the lease extended?"

"Absolutely."

"And Talbot? Is he committed to perpetuating your father's good will?"

"I don't know. But my father owned and leased that land before he partnered with Talbot, so it really doesn't matter."

"When they did become partners, it is likely that their properties were consolidated. If it was agreed between them that the surviving partner acquire sole ownership of the company, how Talbot feels about charity *does* matter. If the land became available for private development, there are fortunes to be made. And anyone intent on getting a stake in the goldmine could have considered your father an obstacle. Including Talbot."

"I don't know how questions of individual holdings were addressed when they partnered, or do I know what provisions are contained in my father's Last Will. I won't know until the document is read at a hearing, and I am not sure when that will be. But whatever my father may leave me, I would trade it all for a chance to go with him to one more baseball game. And, if I am given any say in the matter, I'll do all I can to ensure that the families at Bayshore Heights Village do not lose their homes.

"You asked me to consider suspects, and now you tell me the list could be endless. I can't see how all this guesswork is doing us any good. We seem to be chasing our tails. I have known Talbot all my life. He appeared genuinely distraught at the funeral service and burial this morning. I can simply ask him if he intends to extend the lease."

"I don't think confronting Talbot is a good idea," I said.

I could not remember ever seeing someone's demeanor change so dramatically.

"When I offered to hire you, it wasn't to find out what you *think*. And it certainly wasn't for your advice. You've offered no verifiable proof that your friend did not actually kill my father. Do me a favor. Think what you need to think, and do what you think you need to do, but leave me out of it."

I was about to tell her that all the verifiable proof I needed was Vinnie's word, when she rose from the bench and walked away.

21

They met at the Marina Inn near Oakland International Airport.

"I guess Lockhart made a real mess of things."

"That's an understatement," Bailey said. "Where did you find that moron?"

"He was a psychopath. He seemed perfect."

"A perfect screw-up. First you enlist a maniac, and then you use me to clean up the mess. If you would have given me the Hanover hit to begin with, you would be sleeping better at night."

"I thought his death in a failed robbery would cause less scrutiny than a straight-up execution."

"And how is that working out for you?"

"Is Diamond going to be a problem?"

"I don't believe so. I got all I could from him. All he has is his friend's word. Otherwise, he's running around in circles and clutching at straws. I can't picture him selling his premise to anyone who matters, and I won't be seeing Diamond again. How long until I receive my compensation?"

"It shouldn't be much more than a week, two at the most."

"If I don't see payment in three weeks, I will be back. And I *will* find you."

"Don't worry."

"That's what Bobby Lockhart said."

"You said Lockhart took something from the house. Did you bring it?"

Bailey reached into her satchel and pulled out a plastic bag.

"I wiped it clean of all prints. Do what you like with it, I have no use for a miniature angel statue."

"I prefer leaving it here with you."

ANGEL

I saw the angel in the marble
and carved until I set it free.
—Michelangelo

22

The following day was the last day of September.

I woke up to a wet and chilly Thursday morning.

The kind of weather that often inspired me to stay in bed.

So, I did.

And continued following the exploits of David Copperfield.

Dicken's had recently introduced me to Uriah Heep.

Perhaps it was Heep's manipulation and betrayal of Wickfield that fueled my suspicions regarding Jefferson Talbot.

But, of course, that didn't make those suspicions any less plausible.

And, if Talbot was guilty of treachery—was in any way responsible for or knowledgeable about what actually went down in Hanover's study that night—being questioned by Hanover's daughter could serve as a warning, and could compel Talbot to fortify his defenses.

When I finally reached the office, Darlene was at her desk.

There was a spanking new rawhide bone taking up most of the space at her feet.

Though not quite as large as Rhode Island, the thing looked a lot like a Louisville Slugger.

"How did dinner go?" Darlene asked.

"It was a disaster."

"Did they overcook the seventy-five-dollar Acquerello Car-naroli risotto?"

"I advised Jennifer not to confront Talbot about Bayshore Heights."

"And?"

"She wasn't interested in my counsel, and she said we were through."

"Never tell a woman who can afford dinner at Quince what she should or *shouldn't* do. Did you ask about her brother?"

"Never had the chance."

"Maybe I can find something about Richard Hanover on the internet."

I decided to visit the hospital.

To impress upon Vinnie the great importance of delaying any *out-of-bed* adventures for as long as possible.

Once again, I had Frances waiting—so I could talk with Vinnie alone.

"The longer you pretend you are too weak to get out of bed, the longer it will take them to get you into court for an arraignment. And that will delay an indictment."

"What happened to finding Bobby Lockhart?"

"Lockhart is dead. Murdered."

"Fuck me. When?"

"Monday."

"Why did you wait so long to tell me?"

"I wish I could have waited longer. I didn't see how the news would do anything for your peace of mind."

"Who would have killed Bobby?"

"Probably whoever sent him to kill Hanover."

"What are you talking about?"

"Vinnie, it's a long story. I'll give you the whole picture later. Now, your mother is out there climbing the walls. She's camping out at your place."

"Since when?"

"Since last night. She wants the apartment ready when you are able to go home."

"I hope she rented a Shop-Vac. Why am I always the last one to hear what's going on?"

"Take a wild guess. Look. I promise I will tell you everything I know next time I visit, and keep you in the loop going forward. Meanwhile, make painful noises whenever a nurse simply helps sit you up."

"I'm really worried, Jake."

"I know, buddy. I don't know what more I can say but *hang tough*. It's going to be an uphill battle, Vinnie, but we'll win. Trust me."

"Trusting you is easy, Jake, there is no one I trust more. But knowing my luck, it's fate I have difficulty trusting."

I was headed back to the office when Johnson called.

Johnson told me he had something, so I ran over to the Vallejo Street Station.

"We received a preliminary report from McDonough."

"Remind me?"

"They are checking the items in Hanover's home against the inventory they had conducted a little more than a week ago."

"Right."

"So far, they have been able to identify one item on the earlier inventory that they can't locate in the house."

"So far?"

"They began late yesterday afternoon and plan to be there most of the day today to complete their work."

"A painting?"

"An angel."

"An angel?"

"They called it a figurine. A six-inch-tall angel, with extended wings, cast in metal, standing on a two-inch-high stone base."

"Not the most precise description."

"They did mention it was a Bello."

"A Bello?"

"Created by Sergio Bello, a famous artist down in San Diego. That's all we got. More details will follow."

"Is the thing valuable?"

"It had to be appraised for at least five grand or it wouldn't have made their inventory list. That's all I know, Diamond. I will let you know when I know more."

"It could be good news for Vinnie. If something *was* taken from the house that night, it would be evidence that someone else was there."

"Don't get too excited," Johnson said. "Even though the figurine was at the house recently, doesn't mean it was still in the house when Lockhart and Vinnie got there. Hanover could have sold it, given it away, whatever. On top of that, it might still turn up in the house. When you finally locate something you've been searching for, it's always at the last place you look."

"Did you tell Vinnie to stay in bed?" Darlene asked, when I returned to the office.

"I practically had to beg him. He's going stir crazy. Did you get anything on Richard Hanover?"

"He graduated from Balboa High School, and quit college in his second year at San Francisco State."

"Okay."

"That's it."

"That's it?"

"That's all I could find so far. The trail ended at the college. I did find a high school graduation picture. Can you believe you can find almost any high school yearbook from any high school from any year on the internet? A scary thought. My graduation picture was so horrible, I tore the page out of the book and crammed it down the kitchen trash disposal."

"It couldn't have been that bad."

"No? What was the name of that high school you graduated from in Brooklyn, and the year you graduated? I forget."

"Never mind."

"I could dig a little deeper into Richard Hanover, there are several other resources I can try. But it will have to wait. I need to get to Stinson Beach to collect the pooch. What took you so long to get back here?"

"Johnson."

"Did he have anything new?"

"I'm not sure. I need to call Sergio Bello."

"Isn't he the head chef at Acquerello on Sacramento."

"Close. Bello is an artist in San Diego."

"Oh, that Sergio Bello. What about?"

"How about I clue you in after I speak with him?"

"Works for me."

"Could you do me a favor?"

"Jake, I work for you. You don't have to ask for favors. I will if it doesn't take too long."

"Could you find a number for Bello, and get him on the phone for me?"

"I can do that."

I went to the back office.

Five minutes later, Darlene called out from the front.

"Jake, I have Sergio Bello on line one."

We only had one line.

"And I'm out of here," Darlene added.

"Signor Bello," I began, thinking it had a nice ring to it, "my name is Jake Diamond."

"How may I help you?"

"Do you remember a figurine you made for Frederick Hanover? An angel on a pedestal."

"Of course. One of my finest pieces."

"I need some information about the piece. I was told you could help."

"Frederick could tell you anything I could tell you about the figurine."

"Unfortunately, Frederick Hanover passed away."

"That's terrible news, may I ask what happened?"

"All I can tell you is it was quick," I said, "which can often be a blessing."

"And what exactly is your interest?"

"Estate purposes."

"What would you like to know?"

"How much would you say it is worth?"

"Worth?"

"If you were to give it a monetary value."

"That is very subjective, as with all art."

"Rough figure?"

"Prices of precious metals and stones fluctuate daily. And both platinum and jade have increased in value over the years since I made the piece. I would estimate the platinum at fifty thousand dollars in today's market and the jade near the same. Then, above the value of the materials, is the fact that it is one-of-a-kind. And a Bello."

"Of course. So, it could bring more than one hundred thousand dollars."

"Bring?"

"If it were auctioned, for example."

"Frederick commissioned the figurine as a special gift for his wife. I am sure it held great sentimental value. He would never have thought of parting with it. I hope it remains in the family, as I am certain Frederick would have wished."

"I'm sure it will stay with the family. This is just a formality. Do you have a picture of the angel?"

"I have professional photographs taken of all my work."

"Could you send me a photograph?"

"Certainly. But why ask for pictures sent when you can

simply take a photograph? And why call me for an estimate? I assume you are in San Francisco."

"I am."

"Any licensed appraiser up there could give you a much more accurate assessment of its value."

I have found that asking someone if *they* can be trusted often helps to gain trust, so I gave it a shot.

"Can I be candid with you, sir, and count on your discretion?"

"Certainly."

"The figurine seems to be missing."

"Lost?"

"Or stolen."

"That is very unfortunate, but now I believe I know what you are really asking. What it would bring to someone who wanted to market it."

"Yes."

"Much less than it is worth. And it would not be easy to sell. Trying to move a piece as unique as that would attract a lot of attention. I don't know that I can be of any further help. If you give me a mailing address, I will send the photographs overnight delivery."

"Thank you, you've been a great help. I'm sorry I misled you."

"I'm sure you had your reasons. Please let me know if the figurine is found."

I left the office, picked up a six-pack of Peroni on my way home, ordered a pizza delivery, watched the Giants play the Padres, read several chapters of *David Copperfield*, and hit the hay.

And another day was gone.

They say time flies when you're having fun.

What they don't tell you is it also flies when you're having no fun.

23

I ran out to the hospital first thing Friday morning.

As I left the elevator, I bumped into Frances Stradivarius.

"I don't know what's wrong with Vincent, Jake. Every time a nurse or a doctor as much as touch him, he reacts as if he was stabbed with an ice pick. And every time I walk into his room, he's asleep."

"He'll be fine, Frances. Trust me."

"I'm going down for coffee. Can I bring you something?"

"No thank you, I can't stay long. I'll just pop in on Vinnie for a minute."

When I walked into the room, Vinnie was lying very still with his eyes shut tight.

"It's me, Vin, your mother went down for coffee."

His eyes popped open.

"Good work," I said.

"How long do I need to keep this up?"

"If you can last until after lunch, we'll be good through the weekend."

"You promised that the next time you saw me you would tell me the whole story."

"Vinnie, it would take a while and you need to keep the feigned sleep thing going. Give me a pass for now. Did Angelo send food over?"

"Meatballs. It was the best thing that's happened to me in a week."

"I'll send more, I have to run."

I left the room as Frances arrived.

"Did you talk with him, Jake?"

"He's fast asleep. I didn't want to wake him. I'll check back later."

Darlene was already at her desk, running at full throttle.

Tug McGraw was back under her desk working on his new prize.

"These came, special overnight delivery," she said, handing me two eight-by-ten color photographs. "It's beautiful, but what is it?"

"Something that may have been removed by Lockhart from Hanover's home last Saturday."

I looked at the two photos, taken from front and back of the figurine. I am not much of an art connoisseur, but there was no missing the beauty and delicacy of the work.

"Are you ready to hear the morning news?" Darlene asked.

"Why not."

"Do you want the bad news or the not so bad news first?"

"Not so bad."

"Johnson called. Vinnie won't be arraigned until after the weekend. The bad news is the arraignment has been set for Tuesday morning, rain or shine. I suppose it gives us several more days at least."

"Terrific, several more days of having absolutely no idea about what the hell to do next."

"Jake."

"What?"

"Take a deep breath."

I did.

"Good," Darlene said. "Are you ready for me to continue?"

"Sure."

"I discovered that after quitting college, Richard Hanover enlisted in the Marines. He was deployed to the Middle East. That is as far I as I got, I guess it doesn't help much."

"It's just the way our luck is going, and I don't know that it will change."

"You can't be giving up."

"I'm out of ideas, Darlene. I thought about questioning Jefferson Talbot, but I can't imagine why he would agree to speak with me."

"It can't hurt to ask," Darlene said, putting the phone on speaker and dialing a number she had sitting on her desk. "It's often the simple solution."

The call was answered on the third ring.

"Talbot and Hanover, this is Molly."

"Molly, this is Darlene Roman. Diamond Investigations. We were hoping Jefferson Talbot might find some time to speak with Jake Diamond today."

"Can you hold for a minute?"

"Absolutely."

A minute later, Molly was back on the line.

"Would eleven work? Here at our office?"

"It would work perfectly. Thank you, Molly. Have a nice morning."

Simple as that.

"You might want to prepare," Darlene suggested.

"Prepare?"

"Decide exactly what you hope Talbot can tell you. He may have agreed to meet with you, but it doesn't mean he'll sit around all day waiting for you to get to the point."

"What would I do without you, Darlene?"

"Perish the thought."

On my way out to see Talbot, I stopped at Darlene's desk.

"I was thinking of bringing a photo of the figurine along, in case the need arises."

"What's stopping you."

"It's too large to get into my pocket, and I'd hate to fold it up."

"Front and back view?"

"Just the front should do."

"Do you have a *charged* cell phone on you?"

"Yes."

"Hand it over."

I handed her my cell phone.

She snapped a photo of the photograph.

"There you go."

24

Molly sent me back to Talbot's office.

The office door was open.

"Come in," Talbot said, rising from his desk. "Please shut the door behind you."

He crossed the room and gave me a firm handshake.

"Jefferson Talbot," he said. "You can call me Jeff. May I call you Jake?"

"Sure."

"Good. Please take a seat, Jake."

We both sat.

"I may have to cut this meeting short, Jake, so in the interest of saving time let me begin. I know who you are. I know the man suspected of killing Frederick Hanover is a friend of yours. I am also aware you don't believe your friend is guilty. What I don't know is what I can do for you."

"My friend's name is Vinnie. He couldn't kill a cockroach. He captures them and sets them free in the wild. Vinnie told me that a man named Bobby Lockhart lured him to the house under false pretense, and Lockhart shot both him and Hanover."

"I don't know any more about what happened last Saturday night than what I have read in the newspaper or heard on radio or television. And, your friend's guilt or innocence is not for me to decide."

I cut to the chase.

"In the interest saving time," I said, taking out my cell phone, "do you recognize this?"

I brought up the picture of the angel figurine and showed it to Talbot.

"I know it well. It was a gift from Frederick to his wife, and it was very dear to him. I have been to his home countless times and, ever since Angela passed away, I have always seen the angel sitting on the desk in his study."

"I spoke to Sergio Bello, the artist who made the figurine. Bello said he could not imagine Hanover ever parting with it. Could you?"

"No. Frederick would have never thought of it."

"Yet it was not on his desk when the police arrived at the scene, and it hasn't been located."

"He may have placed it elsewhere. You believe Lockhart took the angel?"

"Yes."

"But nothing else?"

"So far, they have not identified any other missing objects."

"I know the figurine has monetary value. I would estimate the platinum and jade to be worth seventy-five to one hundred thousand dollars. But there are a number of items in the house far more valuable. Why would anyone with robbery in mind take only the angel figurine?"

"Exactly. And my answer is that Lockhart didn't go there to rob Hanover. He was there for one purpose, to kill Hanover— and I believe someone hired Lockhart to do *that* and taking the angel was an afterthought. Which leads me to the question I really came here to ask. Who might have wanted Frederick Hanover dead?"

"I couldn't imagine," Talbot said. "I have never known anyone as well-liked as Frederick."

"Could it have anything to do with Bayshore Heights Village?"

"I don't follow."

"The lease to the land runs out in a couple of months. If the lease is not renewed, the homes of hundreds of working-class families are in jeopardy. On the other hand, if it's not renewed the value of the land for private development is immeasurable."

"Frederick was fully committed to extending the lease. And I was totally supportive. In fact, we were planning to make the announcement at the San Mateo County Board of Supervisors open public meeting next week."

"Will you be making the announcement yourself?"

"When I know I can, I definitely will."

"When you know you can?"

"When Frederick and I formed the partnership, we consolidated our holdings under Talbot and Hanover ownership. All except the property at Bayshore Heights. When his Will is read, we will know if the property goes to the company or to one or more named beneficiaries. The property *is* extremely valuable. We have been approached by many speculators, more often as the lease comes closer to expiration. But we have always stated very clearly, I as adamantly as Frederick, that the lease *would* be renewed. So be assured, the families at Bayshore will not be displaced if I have anything to say about it."

"Who might the named beneficiaries be?"

"Frederick never discussed that with me."

"His son and his daughter surely."

"I would think neither."

"Why not?"

"I see you have done your homework, but it seems you don't know why Richard Hanover suddenly dropped out of college and enlisted in the Marines."

"I *don't* know."

"The Hanover's were a perfect family. Frederick was the personification of success. Angela was smart and beautiful. They loved each other deeply, and loved their children. Richard was a fine young man. He worshipped his father. His one ambition was to be like Frederick, and join the business. Jennifer was remarkable. Gorgeous, intelligent, and an accomplished athlete. And

Jennifer was the light of her father's life.

"When Richard was in his sophomore year of college, studying to be Frederick's protégé, he shared a flat close to the university with three other students. For Richard's nineteenth birthday, his parents planned a special dinner at their home. After dinner, Richard had plans to attend a birthday party his roommates had arranged.

"Jennifer wanted to go with Richard, but Frederick was against it. The partiers would all be college age, there would surely be drinking, and Jennifer was seventeen years old. Jennifer pleaded, but Frederick would not allow her to go. She surrendered. She said she had reading to do for school and went to her room.

"When Richard left thirty minutes later, Jennifer was waiting at his car.

And he took her along.

"Later in the evening, Jennifer needed to get home. Richard had been drinking and was in no condition to drive. He asked one of his roommates to give Jennifer a ride. The roommate was in no better shape. He crashed into a parked vehicle on Geary Street. The driver was killed instantly, and Jennifer was very badly injured.

"Frederick blamed Richard. He banned Richard from their home, and cut off all contact. Angela begged her husband to reconsider, but Frederick was immovable. Richard dropped out of the university, and he enlisted. He was deployed to Kuwait. I have never heard anything about him since then, whether or not he ever came back, and I don't believe Frederick or Angela did either. In any event, Richard was dead to his father. I don't see him figuring into Frederick's will."

"And Jennifer?"

"Her parents were devastated, particularly her mother. Angela was never the same, she had bouts of depression, and she died several years later. While his wife was alive, Frederick took her to visit Jennifer at least twice a week."

"Visit?"

"The Independent Living Center in Berkeley. She had suffered severe physical damage, and diminished mental capability. Jennifer had difficulty recognizing her parents when they visited, and Frederick could not handle seeing her in that condition. After Angela died, he stopped visiting."

I could think of nothing to say.

"Now, you will have to excuse me. I need to attend to other business," Talbot said. "If and when you can convince me that Frederick Hanover was *marked* for death, I will do everything I can to help you follow it through."

I thanked Jefferson Talbot and left.

All the way back to my office my mind bounced back and forth between two questions.

Why bad things so often happened to good people.

And who took me to dinner at Quince, if it wasn't Jennifer Hanover.

25

Before reaching our office, I changed direction and headed out to the Embarcadero.

I walked into Quince. There was a good-sized lunch crowd.

Since I wasn't wearing my custom-made Italian suit, the maître de looked at me as if he thought I was lost.

"If you care to dine, sir," he said, "a jacket and tie are required."

"My name is Jake Diamond. I am a private investigator. I am here to ask a few questions and if you do not answer, I will assume you are hard of hearing and that I will need to raise my voice."

"Please, follow me."

I followed him to an office in back.

"Please have a seat. How can I help you?"

"I was here Wednesday evening. The woman I dined with gave me a credit card to take care of our dinner bill, which I did. I need information about that card."

"To whom did you give the card?"

"To our waiter, who by the way never asked me for identification."

"Mr. Diamond, we cater to a very exclusive clientele. We do not ask for identification, because it would be insulting. If the card clears, it is enough."

Whenever I used *my* card, for as little as a loaf of bread and a gallon of milk, the supermarket cashier *demanded* ID.

"And, I cannot give out information about a client's credit card unless compelled by someone with more authority than a private investigator."

I left without thanking him, and went to try my luck at the Hotel Griffon.

The young lady at the registration counter was more helpful.

She was able to tell me that Jennifer Hanover had checked out Thursday morning.

She was also able to tell me the bill had been paid with a card.

Since I had not even looked at the card the imposter handed me at the restaurant, I could only assume it was the same.

"Can you tell me about the card she used?"

"For that kind of information, you would need to speak to my supervisor. I'm sorry."

"No need to be, I understand. I assume that when someone uses a card you check to be sure it will cover the charges for services."

"Of course."

"And I assume you would still have the card information."

"Yes, but as I said, I couldn't help you with that."

"My name is Jake Diamond," I said, showing her my ID. "What is your name? If you don't mind."

"Laura."

"Laura, maybe you *can* help me," I said. "The card was good when she used it yesterday, is there a way you could determine if it would be good today? You would not be giving me any particulars, just letting me know if the card is still valid. Can you possibly do that? I promise no one will hear of it, and it could be of great help to someone who needs all of the help he can get."

"Someone you care about?"

"Someone I care a great deal about. A very good friend. Someone who would not hesitate to help another."

"Give me a few minutes," Laura said, moving to the computer terminal.

When she came back to me, she was all smiles.

"I can help you without breaking any rules. The card used was a cash card. It is usually used by people who are travelling abroad, because it can be used anywhere in the world. It is like a pre-paid phone card. It's good only for the amount deposited onto it. It covered the hotel charges yesterday, but today it could be worthless."

"Do you need identification to acquire such a card?"

"No. If you funded it with cash, you could say you were Bart Simpson."

Brilliant. A perfect way to cover one's tracks.

"I can't thank you enough, Laura, but I would like to offer you a little something to show my appreciation," I said, reaching for my wallet.

"That's not necessary, Jake. I hope I have done your friend some good."

I stopped into Molinari's for something to eat.

Angelo Verdi heaped hot chicken parmigiana onto a half-loaf of Italian bread, wrapped it in waxed paper, and twisted both ends.

I walked up to headquarters and retreated to the back office.

Darlene had left a note on my desk. Call Sergeant Johnson.

I weighed my priorities. Call Johnson immediately and let the sandwich go cold. Or not.

The chicken parmigiana won.

Johnson was at the station.

"I thought you might want to know that the angel figurine never turned up, they're listing it as missing."

"Darlene is out with the dog. She should be back any minute."

"Good to know."

"Do you have time right now to drop by the office?"

"Are you trying to avoid Lopez?"

"I saw Jefferson Talbot this morning."

"What's the story?"

"That's the thing. If you were here when Darlene gets back, I wouldn't have to tell it twice."

"I'll walk over, give me fifteen minutes."

Darlene and the pooch arrived five minutes later.

"What happened with Talbot?"

"You won't believe it."

"He offered us paid work?"

"Johnson is on his way over. I'll tell you both when he gets here."

I related the Hanover family tragedy, followed by an account of my failed attempt to locate the counterfeit daughter.

"She's in the wind, and I don't have any brilliant ideas about how we could possibly find her. But there *is* the figurine."

"What about it?" Johnson asked.

"Both Sergio Bello and Jefferson Talbot were convinced that Frederick Hanover would never have sold it or given it away. Talbot said that it always sat on Hanover's desk. I have no doubt any longer. Lockhart carried it away. And since it wasn't found in his place, locating the figurine may be the only chance we have left to clear up this mess Vinnie is in."

"If I had a picture of the thing, I could send it out to all of the city police precincts in the Bay Area—and to the state police and county sheriffs—with a BOLO," Johnson said.

Darlene picked up the front view photograph of the angel and passed it to the sergeant.

"Here you go."

"About Vinnie," I asked, "assuming he is arraigned on Tuesday."

"There is nothing to assume," Johnson said. "Vinnie *will be* arraigned Tuesday if they have to carry him into the courtroom on a stretcher."

"And then?"

"He will be under arrest and bail, if granted, will be set. And as soon as the doctors say he can leave the hospital, he'll be locked up unless his bail is covered. In either case, he will be facing indictment. As early as Wednesday, and no later than next week. He needs a lawyer at the arraignment, to argue bail. A very good criminal attorney. I need to be back at the station, I will get this photo out today," Johnson said, heading for the office door. "I would say *good luck,* but it's going to take a lot more than that."

"Where are we going to find a very good criminal attorney in three days?" I asked Darlene, when Johnson was gone.

"I have only one suggestion, and you won't like it."

"Tony Carlucci?"

"Tony Carlucci."

26

Saturday morning.

I sat across the table from Tony Carlucci at Pat's Café on Taylor Street.

Not long before, I had done a favor for Tony and his brother, John.

Their cousin Guido's son, Benny Carlucci, was arrested when he was found in a stolen car with a corpse in the trunk.

Benny swore he had no knowledge of the dead body, Tony asked me to find out how the body got there. I really didn't do much but, when Benny was cleared, "Johnny Boy" rewarded me with a custom-made Italian suit—making the arrangements for the fitting from his prison cell at San Quentin.

When a Carlucci asked for a favor, it was compulsory.

The upside was that their code demanded they return the favor.

I had to wait until Tony had polished off his Polk Street omelet before bringing up business.

I told him what I needed.

"Do you remember Lionel Katz?" he asked.

I did. Katz was the attorney who had represented Benny. He was one of the most well-known criminal attorneys in California.

"I do. But my understanding is that Katz's only client is the Carlucci family."

"My brother will tell him it's family business," Tony said. "Where is your friend, Vinnie?"

"Saint Francis Memorial."

"I'll see to it that Lionel visits him Monday. I'll let you know what time he plans to arrive, if you want to be there."

I would need to be there, since I had more in the way of reasonable doubt than Vinnie himself could offer.

"Thank you, Tony."

"No problem," Carlucci said, with a smile that read *now you owe us one.*

It was another rainy day.

I was dressed with nowhere to go and nothing to do.

Since I was only a few blocks from the office, I walked over to check for phone messages. Darlene had made it clear that after three days juggling our check book, she would not be back at her desk until Monday morning.

There was a voice message from Tom Romano, asking me to call him back.

I wondered why he hadn't called my cell phone, and then realized I had left the cell plugged into the wall at home.

"How about we watch some baseball and play some pinochle? I just spoke to Ira, and he's in."

Tom Romano and Ira Fennessy were fellow private investigators.

We tried to get together for a card game every week or two.

A Saturday afternoon contest was not the norm, but the nasty weather made it sound like a decent alternative to getting wet for no good reason.

The Giants were playing the second of three games in Los Angeles that afternoon, the final games of the season. If the Giants managed to sweep the Dodgers, both teams would finish with the same record and force a one-game tiebreaker to determine the division title.

I told Tom I would be at his place for the first pitch at one.

"I might have some more work for you," Tom said. "I'll know after the weekend. How did it go with Josephine Leone and her wayward son?"

"It saved the day."

We dealt hands and watched the baseball game simultaneously, until the Giants scored a run in the top of the seventh inning and extended their lead to three-zip. We left the card table and gave our undivided attention to the drama unfolding at Dodger Stadium.

Giants' pitching kept Los Angeles scoreless through eight.

In the bottom of the ninth, a few hits and three walks tied the game at three. With one out and the bases full, Steve Finley hit his thirty-sixth home-run of the season. The Dodgers won 7-3, and the 2004 season was all over for Barry Bonds and the gang.

At six, Ira had to leave, so we broke up the card game.

Romano announced he had one extra ticket for the game the next day between the St. Louis Rams and the 49ers.

"If you are both interested, you can flip a coin or draw for high-card."

"I can't," Ira said, "I promised my mother I would come for dinner."

Which reminded me that I hadn't seen my mother for some time, and had me wondering why Darlene hadn't reminded me by now.

"Diamond?" Tom asked, after Ira took off.

"Yes?"

"The football game?"

It was game four of the regular season. Maybe the Niners could manage to finally win one.

And I had no other plans.

Again.

"Sure."

"How about we meet at Monster fifteen minutes before kickoff?"

"Monster?"

"Do you ever read a newspaper or watch the news, Jake?"

"I leave that to Darlene."

"A week ago, they renamed Candlestick Park. It's now called Monster Park."

"For Halloween?"

"For Monster Cable."

Another professional ballpark named for the highest bidder.

Nothing was sacred.

I told Tom I would meet him there.

The remainder of that Saturday evening closely resembled Thursday evening.

Instead of ordering pizza, I picked up a Super Beef Burrito at La Taqueria on Mission Street. And a six-pack of Corona instead of Peroni.

Since that ship had sailed, instead of watching baseball I watched the remake of *The Manchurian Candidate* on HBO.

I'm a Denzel fan, but I couldn't see how it added anything to the 1962 original with Sinatra. And no one could hope to surpass Angela Lansbury's portrayal of pure evil.

I ended the day as I had usually done lately, with a few chapters of Dickens.

Uriah Heep had made the double-cross his art.

Heep had gained Wickfield's trust, and then he stabbed Wickfield in the back.

Heep's treachery is finally exposed by Micawber, a most unlikely hero with nothing to gain and everything to lose.

The kind of unforeseen savior Vinnie Strings could have really used right about then.

27

Sunday morning, Darlene called while I was searching for my Joe Montana jersey.

"When was the last time you saw your mother?"

There it was.

"I'm not sure."

"Fifteen days ago."

"If you knew, why did you ask?"

"It was a test. What are your big plans for today?"

"I'm going to the 49ers game with Romano. Did you know that Candlestick is now Monster Park?"

"Yes. I also heard the Montreal Expos are moving to Washington, D.C. next season and the first presidential debate was last Thursday night. Call your mother. Offer to take her to dinner after the game. Suggest that place she likes close to her house. You know the one, unlimited soup and salad."

"There's something to look forward to."

"Don't sweat. She will insist on cooking, that is if you call now and give her time. I'll go with you, if you need company."

"I can always use backup when I visit Mary. I'll tell her to expect us at five. I'll pick you up."

"You are a model son, Jake. Enjoy the game, maybe the Niners can finally win one."

I called Mary.

Mom insisted on cooking dinner.

She was very pleased Darlene would be joining us.

"I'll make sure there's no meat," she added.

Since the menu would include her legendary eggplant parmigiana, and no tofu, I would survive.

Mary told me five would be fine.

I told her I would bring bread and wine.

I called Darlene, and asked her to be ready at four-thirty.

The Rams won, 24-14, and the 49ers went to 0-4.

Over dinner, I filled Mary in on Vinnie's situation.

"How is Frances?"

"Much better knowing her son is going to be alright physically, but very worried about what he is facing. As we all are."

"And you say Vincent was deceived by a friend?"

"An acquaintance, at least."

"And has this acquaintance been questioned about it?"

"He's dead. Murdered."

"That's terrible."

"He was not a good person, Mom. He brought it upon himself."

"I was thinking of *his* mother. Losing a child is a horrible thing, angel or devil. Family is family. Which reminds me, I have something for you."

Mom went back to her bedroom, returned with three black and white photographs and handed them to me.

"I sent several to your brother in Atlanta," she said.

They were photos of my father with some of his Army comrades in Korea.

I had never seen them.

I passed them to Darlene.

"Can you pick out Jacob's father?" Mary asked.

"Easily. Jake looks a lot like him. Though not as handsome as your husband, of course," Darlene said playfully.

"Those photos are more than fifty years old," I said. "I'm

surprised you still have them."

"Every soldier has pictures of himself and those he fought beside. They end up in a shoebox with his mother, or wife, or children. I thought you might like having these."

"I do. Thank you, Mom."

"I made dessert. Ricotta cheesecake."

"Where do you find the time?" I asked.

"I have plenty of time, Jacob."

I decided I would make it my business to see Mary more often.

Tony Carlucci called later that Sunday night with word that Lionel Katz would be at Saint Francis Memorial Hospital at ten the following morning.

I planned to be waiting there when Katz arrived.

28

When Lionel Katz stepped out of the hospital elevator, I nearly didn't recognize him.

The last time I had seen Katz, he was wearing an Italian virgin wool suit that could have easily matched the cost of a first-class round-trip plane ticket to Milan. And it would have been no surprise to learn he had flown first-class to Milan to have it fitted.

Today, Lionel was wearing matching sweat pants and sweat shirt and running shoes. Of course, the sweats were Brunello Cucinelli and the shoes Givenchy.

I led him to the visitor's lounge for a sit-down.

I told Katz everything I knew, thought I knew, imagined, and guessed about Vinnie's predicament. He took an occasional note.

"Quite a story," Katz said, when I had wrapped it up. "I will need to sift through all of it and try to find one argument that doesn't sound like a shot in the dark. What you've given me is not much stronger than what I have heard from other clients when they say, *okay, I shot the guy, now do your job.*"

I could picture Johnny Boy or Tony Carlucci saying just that.

"What's your plan," I asked, hoping he had one.

"For now, I will put all of my efforts into a reasonable setting of bail and delaying the indictment. If this case ever comes to trial, I will need a lot more than *what ifs* to help keep your friend out of prison."

"Would you like to speak to Vinnie?"

"Does he know anything you haven't told me?"

"No."

"Then, it's not necessary," Katz said, ending the meeting. "I'll see you tomorrow morning in court."

After Katz left, I sat alone for a while. Debating.

Give Vinnie the whole picture of the serious jam he was in, or let him hear about it at the arraignment in the morning.

I decided he should hear it from a friend.

I left Vinnie and was heading for my car when Darlene called.

"Get to the office. Pronto," she said.

When I arrived, I found Sergeant Johnson there with Darlene.

"Recognize this woman?" he said, handing me a photo.

"She's looked better," I said.

It was the Jennifer Hanover impersonator.

"She was discovered shot to death at the Mission Inn near the Oakland Airport. We may have never heard about it over here if not the for the BOLO we sent out. The angel figurine was found in the room where she was killed."

"Wow."

It was the best I could do.

"She was identified as Loretta Bailey. A very elusive contract killer out of Chicago. They also found a gun in the room. I figured it wouldn't hurt to check it against the bullet that killed Bobby Lockhart. The ballistics lab should have test results later today. I'll let you know as soon as I hear."

"Another worm in the can," I said.

"But this one will work in Vinnie's favor. The figurine strongly indicates there was someone else in that house when Hanover was killed. Vinnie named Bobby Lockhart. And, if the lab comes back with a match, Lockhart was killed by a hired assassin. The theory that Vinnie and Hanover were alone, and they shot each other, won't be a slam-dunk. A police department investigation into other possibilities will be demanded by the district attorney's office before they rush to indictment and trial. Have you found a lawyer?"

"Lionel Katz."

"I'm impressed. Although if it were up to me, Katz would be behind bars himself. Get this information to him, I'm certain it will help at the arraignment tomorrow."

"Do you think Vinnie is off the hook?"

"Not yet, but the odds of wiggling free have improved. I'll try my best to be assigned to the Hanover case if it goes active, Lopez will back me. It will be up to us to *hook* whoever hired Bobby Lockhart to kill Hanover, hired Loretta Bailey to kill Bobby, and then killed Bailey."

"How do we begin?"

Johnson laid it out for us.

Johnson would concentrate on Loretta Bailey.

Since Bailey's death was the business of the Oakland Police Department, Johnson would reach out to Lieutenant Don Folgueras of the Oakland PD.

The two had worked together before.

Johnson would ask to be as close to the investigation into who killed Loretta Bailey as possible.

We would focus on Bobby Lockhart, and who hired him to assassinate Frederick Hanover.

The high road and the low road.

Two chances of success.

And, since we had agreed we were likely looking for the same person, if we were both successful we could very well meet where the roads crossed.

Johnson left for the Vallejo Street Station.

"She saw it all. She was there when Hanover was killed, when Lockhart was killed, and when Bailey was killed," Darlene said, lifting the photograph of the angel figurine from her desk. "If only she could talk."

CROSSING THE CHICKEN

Why did the chicken cross the road?
Because the road crossed the chicken.
—David Mamet

29

Tuesday morning. Vinnie sat in a wheelchair, beside his attorney.

Darlene, Frances and I sat in the gallery watching a master at work.

Lionel Katz may not have been an ideal role model for the youth of San Francisco, someone you would see about buying a used car, or someone you would introduce to your sister.

But there was no denying Katz was a marvel in a courtroom.

His argument was articulate and economical, and centered primarily on the journey of a platinum angel from the desk in Frederick Hanover's study to the hotel room in Oakland—and the weapon and hired assassin found with it.

"Your Honor," Katz said. "If Vincent Stradivarius is guilty of anything, it is poor judgment. Vincent was a victim of deception, and almost paid with his life. There are too many unanswered questions to justify an indictment of my client for felony murder, and I ask the court and the prosecution to make every effort to answer these questions before proceeding. I also humbly ask the court to reduce the present charges to *alleged* attempted robbery, and waive bail."

"The charges will stand, for the time being" the judge said. "However, an indictment will not be sought until the district attorney has demonstrated that the uncertainties you presented have been thoroughly investigated. Meanwhile your client will remain under arrest, and he will be taken into police custody as soon as he is discharged from the hospital. Then, he will either be incarcerated or released on bail. Bail will be set at ten thousand dollars."

It was a tremendous victory.

It gave us what was most needed.

Time.

Frances was permitted to ride back to the hospital in the ambulance with Vinnie.

We told her we would follow.

I thanked Katz, and asked him about the charges.

"If it can be proved that Bobby Lockhart did what Vinnie said he did, the most serious charge against Vinnie will be attempted robbery. Since he has no criminal record, we can petition the court for probation and community service. I believe he can avoid jail time," Katz said. "So, get to work finding that proof."

Some people have a knack for making difficult tasks sound easy but, as convincing as Lionel Katz could be, I wasn't quite ready to stop worrying.

We were heading out of the courtroom when Jefferson Talbot rose from a bench in back.

"Your friend's lawyer presented compelling arguments," Talbot said, "and I am now inclined to consider the possibility that Frederick was in fact a target. My offer, to help find out who was behind his death, still stands. Let me know if there is anything I can do."

"Has a date for the reading of Frederick Hanover's Last Will been set?" I asked.

"It is scheduled for tomorrow morning."

"Could you share that information with me? What we need more than anything else are possible suspects."

"Yes, I can. I will call you as soon as I learn of the provisions."

When we arrived at the hospital, Darlene and I went in to see Vinnie.

He seemed cautiously encouraged by the results of the court appearance.

I left Darlene and Frances in the room, and tracked down Vinnie's doctor to find out when they were thinking of cutting him loose.

"Vincent recovery has been going extremely well. He is very anxious to get away from us," the doctor said.

"I'm sure it's not personal."

"Regardless. Vinnie's injury was very traumatic. We will still need to monitor him, and will do so at least until the end of the week. Then, we will evaluate his readiness for release on a day-to-day basis. And, he will not be discharged unless we are assured he will not be at home alone."

There was no worry there.

Frances wasn't going anywhere soon.

On my way back to Vinnie's room, Johnson rang my cell.

"I spoke to Don Folgueras at the Oakland PD. He promised to keep me informed on any developments into the investigation of Loretta Bailey's death. The ballistics lab matched the gun found in Bailey's hotel room to the bullet that killed Lockhart."

More ammunition for Lionel Katz.

"I don't know if I can *survive* another week in this place."

Vinnie could be dramatic.

"Hang in, Vin. Time flies. And think what you'll have to look forward to," I said. "You'll have your mother there with you at home. Like your own private nurse."

The look on Vinnie's face assured me I had succeeded in quashing his urgency to get back home.

"By the way. With all the excitement I forgot to tell you that

Rachel, the waitress at The Homestead, visited to see how you were doing. She likes you."

Vinnie didn't say anything, but he did blush.

I was reminded I had told Rachel I would keep her informed of Vinnie's condition.

And since I hadn't spoken to Rachel after she left a message in my voice mailbox, I had never discovered how she had learned Bobby Lockhart's last name.

I decided to try catching her.

30

Timing is everything.

I found Rachel at The Homestead, and she was able to take a short break.

She was glad to hear about Vinnie's improvement, and empathetic about the problems he could still be facing.

"Thanks for getting back to me with Bobby Lockhart's last name," I said. "How did you find it?"

"I asked my co-workers if anyone knew a *Bobby* who had been in here with Vinnie. Our bartender Adam did, and knew Bobby's last name. I don't know if it's important, but Adam mentioned he saw Bobby here with another man the day before I saw him with Vinnie."

"Is Adam working now?"

"That's him at the bar."

I walked over.

I asked Adam about the man he had seen with Lockhart.

"Very straight looking. Clean cut. Not the type you would expect to see with Bobby. They were very animated. When the other man left, Bobby came up to the bar for another drink. I joked with him—asked if the other man was his stock broker. Bobby said the man was an old buddy from the Marines."

"Can you describe the other man in more detail?"

"Tall. At least six-foot. Brown hair. Mid-thirties."

"Did you get a name?"

"No."

"Would you recognize him if you saw him again?"

"Maybe. They were sitting far across the room, near the front door. I couldn't get a very good look at his face."

"If you *think* you see him again, would you let me know? Rachel knows how to reach me."

"Sure."

I went back to Rachel to thank her again.

"Say hello to Vinnie, I'll try to visit soon," she said.

"I will, and I know Vinnie would like a visit very much."

Bobby Lockhart had identified the other man as *an old Marine buddy*.

I remembered what my mother had said, about soldiers saving photos of their comrades.

And how wives and mothers held on to them afterwards.

Since there were no sure bets, I decided to play a longshot.

I visited Bobby Lockhart's mother.

Impersonating a police detective is both disingenuous and risky.

However, rationalization often trumps proper behavior and good sense.

And Margaret Lockhart seemed glad to know *someone else* cared about who killed her son.

"Your son was seen with another man shortly before his death, a man he may have known in the service. Do you know of any of his Marine friends who he may have been spending time with lately?"

"I don't, but he did send pictures from Kuwait of him and some of his friends there."

"Do you have any of those photos?"

"Of course, I saved all of them. Would you like to see them?"

"I would."

She walked off toward the back rooms of the house.

I spotted a framed photograph on the mantlepiece.

Margaret with her little boy.

Her husband was probably in prison already.

Bobby was an adorable five-year-old.

A reaffirmation that even the nastiest adults were cute children once upon a time.

Margaret returned with four photographs.

"Do you know the names of any of these other men?" I asked.

"No, I'm afraid I don't. Bobby may have mentioned names, but I can't recall."

"Could I possibly borrow these for a short time? I promise you will get them back unharmed."

"Would it help find out who killed my Bobby?"

"It might."

"Then, please take them."

I rushed back to The Homestead.

Adam was busy mixing drinks, but he was able to take a quick look at the four photographs.

"All of these men are wearing beards, hats and dark glasses. Honesty, I can't be positive. And I couldn't swear to it if it came to that."

Back in my car, I called Johnson.

"I have photographs of Lockhart and some of the men who served with him in Kuwait, and one of the others might have been seen with Bobby just before Hanover was killed."

"I would ask where you found those photographs, but I probably don't want to know. Take pictures with your phone and send them to me. Do you remember how to do that?"

Surprisingly, I did.

"I'll reach out to my uncle," Johnson said.

"Your uncle?"

"He's a two-star Major General in the Marines. I'll ask him if he can dig up any information on Bobby Lockhart's military record. Men he served with, in a company or a platoon. And I'll send him copies of the photos. I'm sure he will have to cut through a mountain of red tape, but I know he'll try his best to come up with names and identify faces. It could take a while."

Everything was taking a while, but it felt as if we really had something. Finally.

It would do little good if we couldn't identify the man, and were unable to find him.

"Anything from Oakland?" I asked.

"Nothing. Lieutenant Folgueras is requesting the manpower needed to interview hotel employees and guests, with the hope someone may have seen whoever visited Loretta Bailey that night. But it may not be an easy sell."

"Why is that?"

"Like everything else having to do with municipal budgets, it's a matter of cost. There are nearly one hundred full and part-time employees at that hotel, and a few hundred guests were registered at the time. Most of those guests are now scattered throughout the entire country. A canvassing of that magnitude is extremely expensive, and the elimination of a cold-blooded killer like Loretta Bailey could be considered more a benefit than a loss to society. But, speaking of Bailey, it has me thinking."

"What?"

"It's obvious Bailey came to you to find out how much you knew, and posing as Jennifer Hanover was a clever move. But how did she know there was a daughter to begin with?"

"From Hanover's obituary?"

"I'm guessing that Bailey was called in to handle Lockhart *after* Hanover was killed. I doubt she would have seen the obituary. And, there was nothing in the obituary about his daughter's physical condition. Whoever hired Bailey had to know the real

Jennifer wouldn't pop up to blow Bailey's cover."

"And Bailey knew a good deal about Frederick Hanover and his business. About his art collection, about Bayshore Heights Village, Jefferson Talbot, and the funeral she obviously never attended—as if she was schooled by someone who knew their stuff. Does that help us?"

"Probably not a lot. It may narrow the field of suspects. I'll let you know if and when I hear anything from Oakland or my uncle."

"And what should I be doing while we wait?"

"Try narrowing the field a little more. But be careful. Considering what happened to Hanover, Lockhart and Bailey—it's a mine field."

31

When I walked into Diamond Investigations early Wednesday morning, Darlene was already at her desk with news that Tom Romano had called.

"He was hoping we could take another case off his hands," she said. "I asked him *what kind of case?* He said *a piece of cake.* I asked *what kind of cake?* He said *a gentleman who suspects his wife is having an affair.*"

"And you said, *no, but thanks for asking.*"

"In not so many words."

"Way to go."

"My pleasure."

At eleven, while I was sitting in the back office twiddling my thumbs, I received a call from Jefferson Talbot.

Talbot asked if I could come over to his office, so he could relate to me all he had learned from the reading of Frederick Hanover's Last Will.

We decided on a meeting at one.

"Frederick's interest in Talbot and Hanover will remain with the company itself, and its shareholders," Talbot began.

"This does not benefit me personally, except in terms of my

own stock shares—which are modest. This was the arrangement we had agreed upon when we set up the partnership, and it is not a surprise.

"Frederick's liquid assets, nearly two million dollars, will be granted to the Independent Living Center in Berkeley. It will easily cover the expense of Jennifer's care for as long as she lives and, in the event of her death, all that remains will be donated to the facility."

"That's very generous."

"Frederick had always been committed to his daughter's care, but may have harbored guilt about *putting her away*. His wife was against it. Angela wanted to care for their daughter at home. But, as I mentioned the last time you were here, Frederick couldn't handle seeing Jennifer in that condition and after Angela passed away he stopped visiting completely. These were the provisions which were spelled out *specifically* concerning the company, his liquid assets, and his daughter's continued care. The question of his non-liquid assets is not so clear. These include his residence and all its contents—paintings, coin and stamp collections, sculpture—as well as his personal shares of the company."

"Not so clear?"

"The Will was drafted and signed sometime between the auto accident and Angela Hanover's death. Angela was named beneficiary, and Frederick never had the document amended after she passed away which—in effect—is the same as Frederick dying without having named any primary beneficiaries. Therefore, all of his assets which were not specifically granted in the *existing* Will are subject to intestate succession."

"Meaning?"

"The state will determine who inherits based on the strongest claims. In California, if a person dies with children and no spouse, the children are at the top of the list. Next in succession are other immediate family. Siblings, and children of siblings. Nieces and nephews. The state will do all it can to notify the eligible claimants, who will then have sixty days to make a claim. So, in Frederick's case, Richard and Jennifer would be first in line. Followed by his surviving brother and sister, and their children."

"What about Bayshore Heights Village?"

"There were no specific designations, it would be up to whoever is named as primary beneficiary."

"Can I ask about the estimated value of the estate?"

"Nearly four million dollars. I know you are looking for suspects, those who might benefit from Frederick's death. But, I assure you, his brother and sister are out of the question. Robert Hanover is a very successful businessman. He owns a large chain of sporting goods retail stores on the east coast, and his son and daughter work with him. He came out here with his wife for the funeral, appeared sincerely distraught over Frederick's death, and showed no interest in the dispensation of his brother's assets. I don't think he expects anything. He didn't even ask about the Will. Frederick's sister, Charlotte, is a Dominican Sister doing missionary work in Africa. She has no children. I do not believe that either sibling would have motive or opportunity to orchestrate Frederick's death."

"What can you tell me about Jennifer's physical and mental condition?"

"Physically, she is confined to a wheelchair and she requires constant assistance with regard to basic physical requirements. Mentally, Jennifer is limited in the kinds of choices she has the capacity to comprehend and could effectively act upon. For instance, she could decide what she wanted to eat or what she might need at the moment—but she would not be capable of making more complicated decisions with respect to medical or financial matters."

"So, who would make those kinds of decisions for Jennifer?"

"I would guess Frederick had power of attorney."

"And now, with her father gone?"

"There were no stated provisions in the will. Unless there exists a codicil that we are unaware of, I'm not sure. Perhaps the facility where she resides."

"Would you mind one more question?"

"Go ahead."

"Who would know about Jennifer Hanover's medical condition?"

"I really couldn't tell you. Frederick did not openly talk about it."

"I appreciate your time and candor," I said, having run out of questions.

Talbot opened a checkbook, filled in a check, and he handed it across the desk to me.

Five thousand dollars.

"What's this?" I asked.

"One thousand dollars is to cover a bail bondsman for your friend, if it comes to that. And the remainder, I would like to contribute to your efforts to discover if Frederick was in fact targeted for assassination and—if so—who was responsible. Please do not refuse, Jake, and please keep me informed of any progress."

So, I did not refuse.

"And here is my cell phone number," Talbot said, jotting it down on a slip of paper he tore from a small pad on his desk, "in case you can't reach me here at the office."

I promised Talbot I would inform him as soon as I knew more, hoping I would eventually know more.

32

When I arrived at the office Thursday morning, Darlene was at her post.

She was leaning over her desk with a magnifying glass up to her face.

"What's up, Sherlock? Where's the pooch?"

"Spending the day with my father. Take a look at this."

Darlene handed me one of the photographs I had received from Bobby Lockhart's mother.

There were two soldiers. They both wore camouflage military jackets, matching wide-brimmed hats, dark sunglasses, and a good amount of facial hair. I knew Bobby, he was the only one in all four photos.

"Okay."

"Now, take a look at this," she said.

She handed me another picture.

"Do you think this is the same guy?" Darlene asked.

There was a resemblance. But the soldier was several years older, and the young man in the other photo was a clean-cut kid.

The picture looked like the ones we posed for in school, where every teenager looks nearly the same.

"There's a likeness, but I wouldn't bet my sixty-five Impala convertible on it. So, where did *this* picture come from?"

"As you may recall, I printed it off the internet a few days ago."

"Remind me."

"It's Richard Hanover's high school yearbook photo."

I controlled the impulse to jump to conclusions, and instead adopted the voice of reason.

"*Maybe* it is Richard Hanover in the picture with Lockhart, maybe not. *Maybe* Johnson can find out through his uncle if Hanover and Bobby served together, and *maybe* they did. And in any case Adam, the bartender at The Homestead, said *maybe*—adding he would not testify that he could positively identify the man he saw with Bobby. That's a lot of maybes."

"The thing about maybes," Darlene said, "is that they *may be.*"

"The SFPD and the DA won't see it that way. They will pay little if any attention without stronger evidence that Richard Hanover met with Lockhart before Frederick Hanover was killed."

"I think the question is—if the prodigal son suddenly reappeared, why have his father killed? From what we've learned about Hanover's rejection of his son, why would Richard Hanover even imagine he would be named as a beneficiary?"

"He wouldn't."

"So, how does he benefit?"

"As it happens, Hanover never changed his Will after his wife passed away, and she was beneficiary. So now, the two children are next in line for inheritance."

"His children wouldn't have known that was the case, unless they were aware that their father had failed to change his Last Will after his wife's death. I don't see how Richard would know. And, from what I understand, his sister is hardly aware of anything."

"If Richard is truly out of the picture—Jennifer stands to inherit four million dollars in estate property, plus the Bayshore Heights property in San Mateo County which is easily worth ten times that much. Which, sad to say, could be like giving a differentiation of trigonometry functions problem to a five-year-old. Unless..."

"Unless?"

"Grab the pictures. Let's take a ride."

"Where?"

"Berkeley."

We walked from the car to the entrance of the Independent Living Center in Berkeley.

"What's troubling you, Jake?"

Darlene could read me like a road map.

"I'm not sure how we should approach this. These kinds of institutions are famous for confidentiality."

"How about this," she suggested. "You use your charm, and I'll snoop around."

When we entered the building, I went directly to the reception desk and Darlene slipped down the hall.

"May I help you?"

The nameplate on the counter identified her as Theresa Greco.

"A lovely name," I said. "Theresa is my mother's name."

Not honest, hopefully charming.

"Quite a coincidence. So, may I help you?"

So much for that.

"You have a resident, Jennifer Hanover."

"We do."

"Could you tell me who may have visited her lately?"

"I would need to know something about your interest."

"What if I told you I am not permitted to say?"

"Then I would say I am not permitted to tell you."

I realized Darlene and I should have switched tasks. She was much more charming and I wasn't a bad snoop.

"How about if I asked *if* she has had visitors, without asking for names?"

"Jennifer never had *any* visitors for many years until around ten days ago. A man came to visit. He said he was a friend of the family. We were all surprised, and pleased, that finally someone was interested in Jennifer. He's been here for all of our regular visiting hours since he first appeared, and she has reacted positively to the visits. And that's all I can tell you."

"Has he always come alone?"

"In fact, he came yesterday with another man. But I couldn't tell you anything more about the other man either."

"I understand. Thanks for your help."

"Sorry I couldn't say more. By the way?"

"Yes?"

"Is your mother's name really Theresa?"

"Mary."

"Lovely name. And yours?"

"Jake."

"Not bad."

I waited out front for Darlene.

"Get anything?" she asked.

"Not enough. Jennifer has been visited lately by someone claiming to be an old friend. Next visiting hours are on Saturday. We need to stake this place out, look for the long-lost friend to show up again."

"Did you show the photographs?"

"I didn't want to make too much noise. I don't want to alert anyone. I'm hoping the receptionist won't mention my visit. How did you do?"

"I found Jennifer's room, and I caught a woman coming out."

"Oh?"

"Kate. A nursing student at UC, doing volunteer work. I told her I was new to the staff, and hoping to get some initial impressions of how residents were doing."

"And?"

"She told me Jennifer seemed to be doing better since she was getting regular visits."

"Did she say *who* was visiting regularly?"

"Tall, handsome, mid-thirties, impeccably dressed."

"Name?"

"No, but Kate gave me this," Darlene said, handing me a business card. "Yesterday morning, he arrived with a second man. The other man left before he did. In the reception area, he offered Kate his business card. In the event she ever had need of his services."

I looked at the card.

Irving Sulam. Financial Consultant. Notary Public.

"Talk about self-promotion," I said. "We need to talk to this guy. I'll see if I can get Sonny to come along with me, in case Irving is shy."

To those who knew him, Sonny Badalamenti was a gentle soul.

A dedicated husband and father, unhesitatingly generous, and a friend in deed.

When the occasion arose, Sonny could be very persuasive.

Scary persuasive.

Back at our office on Thursday, I gave Sonny a call.

He said he could join me the following morning for a trip to chat with Irving Sulam.

With nothing else on the agenda, I called Tom Romano and Ira Fennessy.

We arranged a pinochle game.

While we played out overbid hands, we watched the Los Angeles Dodgers get beat up by the St. Louis Cardinals in the National League Division Series.

Again.

33

The address on Irving Sulam's business card brought us to a storefront on Washington Street in downtown Oakland on Friday morning.

The sign above the entrance read *Min Jee Nails*.

There was nothing to do but walk in.

At least a dozen women—customers and manicurists—were talking at the same time in a foreign language.

The woman at the front counter was having trouble with my accent, so I showed her the business card.

She directed us to a hallway at the back of the shop.

At the end of the hall, we came to a door with a sign.

Irving Sulam, Esquire.

"Should I do the talking?" Sonny asked.

"Please do."

He handed me one of the masks, and rapped on the door.

A man's voice invited us to enter.

It was a small room, with two folding metal chairs facing a small desk. The man behind the desk was talking on the telephone.

"Please take a seat, I'll be right with you."

We sat.

"So, how can I help you?" he said, when he ended the call and finally looked up at us.

He found himself face to face with Richard Nixon and

Ronald Reagan.

"What is this?" Irving Sulam asked.

"We have some money to invest, we're looking for a financial consultant to give us advice. Excuse the masks, we prefer to remain anonymous for the time being. Think of it as a warm-up for Halloween later this month," Sonny began.

"I really can't help you. My work is mainly involved in helping clients with their income tax returns."

"So. When you went to the Independent Living Center in Berkeley, it was to help Jennifer Hanover with her income taxes?"

"What is this?" he repeated.

"It's called a Q and A, where I ask and you respond."

"And if I don't?"

"Are you going to ask stupid questions or give us smart answers?"

"I should call the police."

"Be our guest, Irving. We can only threaten you. The police have the power to arrest you if you have done something naughty. It is your choice. Trick or treat."

"A man walked in yesterday. He said he was an attorney representing an accident victim and he needed a notary. He offered me three thousand dollars to drive him over to Berkeley with my stamp and my ink pad. We visited one of the residents. He had her sign a document. I witnessed the signing, and then I left him there."

"What was she signing?"

"I didn't read the document. I don't think she did either, but she didn't hesitate. She seemed very willing to please him."

"I'll ask again. What was she signing, Irving?"

"I'm not certain."

"Don't you read through documents when you witness signing?"

"I only need to verify the signature. He asked me not to bother with the details. Three thousand dollars is a lot of money, especially when most of my regular clients are now doing tax returns online for free."

"What was his name?"

"I don't know that either. Or know how to get hold of him."

"I guess you *should* call the police," Sonny said. "I don't see how we can help you."

"Help me?" Irving said.

"Do you mind, Ronnie?" I asked.

"Not at all, Dick," Sonny answered.

I pulled out Richard Hanover's high school yearbook picture. "Is this him?"

"The guy was in his mid-thirties. This is just a boy. I am really not certain."

"Is it possible?"

"It's not impossible."

Maybe. Maybe not.

"But you would know him if you saw him again."

"Yes, but I don't expect to ever see him again."

"You never know, Irving."

"What does that mean?"

"Let me put it simply. You are in deep shit. You could be charged with conspiracy to commit fraud. The amount of money involved would make it a felony. Three thousand dollars wouldn't cover bail. If that isn't enough, you could be in danger."

"What kind of danger?"

"The serious kind. The good news is I think we can help you, but only on one condition."

"What condition?"

"Our word is the law. You do everything we tell you to do, when we tell you to do it, with no argument. Starting now."

It was time for Sonny to take over again.

He reached into his pocket, pulled out what he had tried to explain to me was a throw-away cell phone, and handed it to Sulam.

"First, you will find a place to hide. Immediately. Hotel or motel. Where no one knows you, and no one will know where you are."

"For how long?"

"At least until that phone rings."

"How long might that be?"

"In the immortal words of Irving Sulam, Esquire—I'm not certain."

"What about my wife and children?"

"You're not listening. No one. Hopefully your wife and children will still remember you when this is over. Before you answer one last question, Irving, I strongly recommend your answer is no. Are you going to disappoint us?"

"No."

"Good. Get going."

With that, Sonny rose and I followed.

We removed the masks in the hall, waved goodbye to the women in the salon, and returned to the car.

I called Jefferson Talbot.

"Do you believe Jennifer Hanover would be considered mentally fit enough to designate power of attorney to someone?"

"Possibly, if she understood what she was doing. Has she?"

"I'm not sure yet. I'll get back to you if and when I know more."

"What did we learn?" Sonny asked.

"If it is Richard Hanover, we learned his angle. Not expecting to inherit a penny from his father, he may be arranging to get at it through his sister. He first visited her just after his father was killed."

"That sounds like something premeditated."

"Yes. But no *beyond a reasonable doubt* proof."

"Can we get it?"

"Possibly. But only if he is led to believe we already have it, and he doesn't call the bluff. And first we need to find him. Which means I will be spending a lot of time in my car outside the Independent Living Center with David Copperfield."

34

Visiting hours at the Independent Living Center were Saturday, Sunday, Tuesday and Wednesday from nine to noon and one until four.

Saturday morning Darlene gave me a quick lesson on how to use her digital SLR camera with its 55-250mm telephoto lens.

Angelo Verdi in the deli fixed me up with a scrambled egg, bacon and cheese sandwich on a hard roll for breakfast; a genoa salami, capicola and provolone hero for lunch; a thermos of coffee and two Manhattan Specials.

I sat across Adeline Street watching the entrance and reading.

Emily's trials and tribulations in the saga of David Copperfield had me thinking of Jennifer Hanover.

A beautiful, intelligent, talented young lady standing at a threshold of limitless possibility when the door was closed to her at seventeen.

Abandoned by her father, separated from her mother and—if our worst suspicions were correct—manipulated by her own brother.

And no one came to visit Jennifer on Saturday.

After another fruitless day of surveillance on Sunday, I drove back and stopped into the hospital to visit Vinnie.

"The 49ers finally won a game," Vinnie said, when I walked

into his room. "Thirty-one twenty-eight in overtime. They're cutting me loose on Tuesday."

"Good."

"We'll see. Lionel Katz dropped by. He said he would like you to give him a call as soon as you can."

"I will."

"Any luck in Berkeley? Darlene filled me in."

"Not yet. Where's your mom?"

"You just missed her. She's putting the finishing touches on the new and improved crib in preparation for my return. That is if I don't wind up in the clinker."

"You won't. We have bail covered. Let's see what Katz has on his mind. I'll let you know once I speak with him."

"Rachel from The Homestead came to visit."

"Nice."

"She said she would try to visit when I get home, but I don't think I'm ready for her to meet my mother."

I called Lionel Katz.

We arranged to meet at Caffe Roma on Columbus Avenue at nine on Monday morning.

"Remarkable eggs benedict," Katz said, in way of a recommendation.

I could have mentioned I don't touch eggs unless they are burnt to a crisp, but decided it was too much information.

On top of that, Caffe Roma was one of my favorite Italian bakeries.

I went with coffee and Sfogliatelle.

I was anxious to give Katz the latest.

"I'm almost sure I've found a suspect," I said.

"Suspect?"

"The man behind the death of Frederick Hanover."

"Do you have proof?"

"No."

"Have you mentioned this to the police?"

"No."

"Don't. Without proof, it would only work against my strategy."

"Strategy?"

"I have an appointment set for this afternoon with the assistant district attorney handling Vincent's case."

"Are you going to argue for a lesser charge?"

"No."

"No?"

"Considering Loretta Bailey, the weapon used to kill Bobby Lockhart and the angel figurine found with her body, the prosecution is no big rush to indict Vincent on the charge of felony murder. They are required to demonstrate they have investigated alternative possibilities with due diligence—and they haven't to date. It would be more expedient for the district attorney to indict Vincent on a lesser charge—knowing they can always raise the stakes if and when they can convince the court they have gone through all the motions. So, if we hope to delay an indictment, it is best if the charge is *not* reduced. Of course, the prosecutors understand this—and I am certain they are considering the safe bet. I need to persuade them to let the original charge stand and indefinitely postpone *any* indictment hearing."

"And how do you expect to do that?"

"I will bargain a trade for valuable information I can offer the district attorney, courtesy of John Carlucci."

I could have asked for details, but I didn't want to know.

I found Darlene at her desk at headquarters working on the *Chronicle* crossword puzzle.

"Need help?" I asked.

"What's a seven-letter word for irrigation canal?"

"I have no idea."

"In that case, thanks for the offer—but I guess I'll tough it out on my own. Johnson was trying to reach you, forget your cell phone again?"

"Turned it off while I was meeting with Katz. What did Johnson want?"

"He received some information from his uncle, and thought you would be interested. What did Katz have to say?"

I gave her the short version.

"And, he said we should keep the Independent Living Center business from the police until we have something less sketchy. He's worried that any additional theoretical crime solving will rock the boat."

"Does that include Johnson?"

"I haven't decided what I should tell Johnson. I'll wait until I hear what he has for us."

"Better to receive than to give."

"I'm trying to do what's best for Vinnie. I'm not a big fan of his lawyer's ethics, but Katz knows his craft."

"I get it, Jake. Crafty Katz. I'm sure you'll make the right decision. Go ahead, Johnson sounded anxious."

Johnson waved me over to a chair at his desk.

"Darlene said you heard from your uncle."

"I did."

"Let me guess. Richard Hanover and Bobby Lockhart served together in the Marines."

"They did, in the same company in Kuwait and Iraq. But that's not the half of the half of it."

"Okay."

"During a reconnaissance mission in Iraq, Hanover was separated from his unit. He was not heard from again for a dozen years. The Marines listed him as missing in action, though believing he was more likely a fatality. When he ultimately walked into the American Embassy in Cairo, he claimed that he'd spent the missing years as a POW. The government was skeptical, and he was charged with desertion. Desertion during wartime is treasonous and it could, according to military law, be punished by execution. Since desertion has been a problem in Afghanistan and in Iraq, the government has been trying to instill discouragement. He was held for nearly a year in military prison, while they attempted to build a case for court martial. Hanover could not *prove* he was held prisoner, but the military court couldn't *prove* he was not. Hanover was finally released ten months ago."

"If he *was* a prisoner of war for more than a decade, and he survived only to be welcomed home with incarceration in his own country, I can't imagine the kind of hell he went through."

"My uncle is working on learning the names of other Marines who served with Hanover and Lockhart, starting with those pictured in the photos you got from Lockhart's mother, and he's hoping to find recent photographs. Anything new on your end?"

My relations with Sergeant Johnson had gone from icy, to lukewarm, to he had saved my life recently and was going out on a limb to help me now.

I decided to come clean.

"I believe Katz gave you sound advice" Johnson said. "If we present the prosecutors with more guesswork, it could muddy the waters to the extent they *do* indict Vinnie on a lesser charge. I don't even want to bring it to Lopez. It would put her in a compromising position I am sure she could live without. And I can't help you much, for reasons too many to list. I suggest you continue the stakeout, hope to find out who has been visiting Jennifer Hanover—her brother or otherwise—and then we decide where to go from there."

And that, for lack of a better term, was the plan.

Monday evening, I smuggled two veal parmigiana hero sandwiches and a six-pack of Saint Pauli Girl into Vinnie's room to celebrate his last night in the hospital.

I told him about his lawyer's plans.

"Do you think it's a good idea?"

"I trust Katz's abilities, if nothing else about him. The risk is that if the charge remains felony homicide, and if the police can convince the prosecutor there are no better suspects—and we don't have anything solid to help at this point—they could go ahead and seek an indictment and bail could possibly be revoked. I think it's a sound move and Sergeant Johnson agrees. But I won't lie to you, it is a gamble."

"Well, Jake. If I am nothing else, I am a gambler. Pass me one of those beers."

35

I was back on Adeline Street, across from the Independent Living Center, by nine-thirty on Tuesday morning.

At ten, while I was working on a breakfast burrito, a cab pulled up in front. A tall, well-dressed man in his mid-thirties left the taxi and entered.

He matched everyone's sketchy description.

He was out on the street again at noon, when morning visiting hours were over.

I snapped a few photographs.

The telephoto was perfect for head shots.

He waited until another cab pulled up. I followed the taxi.

The trip was less than two miles, to the Nash Hotel on University.

It was an extended stay hotel. I knew the type—set up for short-term residence. Rooms with kitchenettes, rented by the week or month.

The main building housed the reception area, a restaurant more like a diner, and a small lounge with bar.

Rooms were on two levels, accessed from outdoors, on the street level or second story balcony.

I watched him enter his unit.

I called Tom Romano.

"Do you have anyone I can use to sit on a subject? I usually use Vinnie, but he's on injured reserve. It would be in Berkeley."

"You're in luck. I have a nephew out in Berkeley, Billy, does that kind of thing for me. He takes classes part time and does odd jobs. He wants to be a private eye when he grows up. I keep telling him private investigators aren't grownups, but he's stubborn. I'll try to get hold of him and have him phone you for the particulars."

I called Darlene.

"What's new?"

"I have pork green chili on the front of my shirt."

"Let me rephrase. What's different?"

"I may have spotted our man. I followed him to his hotel. I'm waiting to hear from Romano's nephew, hoping he can be our eyes for a while so I can get out of here."

"Johnson sent photos over. The most recent he could find of the Marines in the patrol unit with Hanover when he disappeared. He was able to dig them up through driver's licenses."

"Terrific. I took some good shots of this guy with your camera."

"If you don't hear from the nephew," Darlene offered, "let me know where you are and I'll bring these photos to you."

Billy called.

He said he was free all day.

I told him where to find me.

He said he would make a quick stop for take-out food, and would get to me in twenty to thirty minutes.

Billy arrived, displaying youthful enthusiasm and a studied command of the jargon.

"Should I tail the mark if he bounces?" he asked, with what I thought was an unconscious Bogart impression.

"I figure he's from out of town," I said, after showing him the photos on the camera and pointing out the unit he needed to be watching. "He has been using taxis, this place is set up for temporary residence, and I believe he's staying low profile. I'm more concerned he may check out, rather than take a stroll. If he calls a cab, follow if you can—and if anyone visits him here, follow the visitor."

"How long would you like me to stay?"

"I'll call you. Can you be available tomorrow?"

"I can be back here first thing in the morning."

"Good."

Back at the office, Darlene uploaded the photographs from the camera to the computer—so we wouldn't have to squint at a three-by-two-inch display to compare them to the driver's license photos Johnson had sent over.

We sat side-by-side at her desk, like two kids waiting to uncover the prize in a Cracker Jack box.

We found the photo Johnson had identified as Richard Hanover.

By no stretch of the imagination was it the same man.

Darlene was first to react.

"Well."

"Well?" I added.

"Mark Twain said, *What gets us into trouble is not what we don't know, it's what we know for sure that just ain't so.*"

"What now?"

"Now, we hope it's one of these other Marines."

And there he was.

Edward Joseph Salerno.

"So," Darlene said, without a trace of sarcasm, "what might we *know for sure?*"

I picked up the blowup of Salerno's driver's license Johnson had sent over.

It had Salerno living in Chicago, Illinois.

If this was our guy, we needed to get something solid before he headed back to the Windy City.

I called the number for the disposable cell phone Sonny had given to the notary, Irving Sulam, hoping he had respected our instructions and remained incommunicado.

"I need to see you. Where are you?"

"Who is this?" Sulam asked.

"One of the men who visited you at the nail salon on Friday."

"The tall one or the short one?"

"I would say the *shorter* one, but what the hell is the difference?"

"How do I know it's you?"

"Because I have this cell phone number and I'm told I look a lot like Dick Nixon. Now, are you going to tell me where you are or do I send Ronnie out to visit your wife and kids? You don't want to know what Reagan would do."

Irving gave it up.

"Find out whatever you can about this guy Salerno," I said to Darlene. "Reach out to Johnson for help. And could you make a copy of this photo and run it out to The Homestead? Show it to the bartender, Adam."

"I thought he said he couldn't be certain."

"It was the beard, hat and dark glasses that gave Adam pause. He might have more confidence in identifying Salerno from this photograph. It's worth a shot."

"Where are you off to?"

"I need to show the photo to the tax consultant."

"While you're at it—ask if we can deduct Camel cigarettes, George Dickel whiskey and dog-eared paperback novels as business expenses this year."

Sonny would never harm an innocent woman or child, but Sulam wouldn't know that and I felt bad about threatening the man's family—so I picked up some food from Molinari's to bring out to the Muir Lodge Motel in Martinez where Irving was holed up.

Sulam had chosen a good hideout.

I had trouble finding the place even with directions.

Irving was overjoyed by the veal parmigiana, baked ziti and caprice salad I delivered. Seemed he had been living on fast food breakfast sandwiches and burgers for the past four days. He said he didn't know how far he was allowed to wander, and he could see the Golden Arches from his motel window.

I showed Sulam the photo of Edward Joseph Salerno.

"That's him."

"Are you sure."

"Positive. What now?"

"You should try chewing that food, it makes it easier to digest."

"What now," he repeated, "can I go home to my family?"

"Have you spoken with your wife?"

"Yes. Before I found this place. I told her I suddenly needed to go out of town on business. She didn't believe a word of it, but at least she won't report me a missing person to the police—which wouldn't do any of us any good."

"You'll be home soon, I'll call you. Meanwhile, stay right here—but you can go further than across the avenue to find something to eat. I need to run. You are doing a good thing, Irving."

"I hope you can help me convince my wife when the time comes."

I called Darlene from the car.

"All I could learn about Salerno is that he's a lawyer with a practice in Chicago. Johnson said he'll try to dig deeper."

"Loretta Bailey was from Chicago."

"Don't get ahead of yourself."

"The bartender?"

"There's the rub."

"Oh?"

"I showed him the photo of Salerno. Adam said *definitely not*. Then I showed him the other driver's license photos Johnson sent over and he picked one out as a *probable*. Max Musman. Lives here in San Francisco. Johnson is having Musman picked up and brought to Vallejo Street Station for questioning."

"Can you call Johnson back and try to sweettalk him into waiting until I get there before he interviews the guy?"

"Why don't you just sweettalk Lieutenant Lopez?"

"Please."

"I'm on it."

Johnson was sitting at a table with Max Musman in an interrogation room.

I was standing beside Lopez in an adjoining room with a one-way mirror and a speaker.

"Do I need a lawyer?" Musman asked.

"I don't know. Let's begin and see how it goes. You were recently seen with Bobby Lockhart at The Homestead."

"Okay."

"What can you tell me about that meeting?"

"I saw more of Lockhart when we first got back from Iraq— I hadn't heard from him in a while. He called and said he needed help, and there was money in it for me. I have a wife and two daughters who don't know the meaning of the words *dress for less*, so money is always worth hearing something about."

"And?"

"He said he had to collect a debt and needed someone to go with him for backup. I didn't like the sound of it, so I passed."

"Did he mention who owed him?"

"No. He dropped the subject. We had a few beers, talked about the only thing we actually have in common—our time in the Corps, the guys we served with, *semper fi* and all that—and I left."

"You served with Richard Hanover and Edward Salerno?"

"Yes."

"Have you had contact with either?"

"Rick went MIA in Iraq—I never heard anything more about him. Last I heard, the Corps sent Salerno through law school.

You should be talking to Bobby. I don't know any more, I don't know what this is all about, and really don't want to know."

"He doesn't know that Bobby Lockhart is dead," Lopez said to me when Johnson had nothing more.

Johnson and Lopez decided to cut Musman loose.

Johnson told me he was waiting to hear from his uncle—hoping to learn more about Edward Salerno.

I went back to the office to talk with Darlene about Plan C or Plan D.

We were getting absolutely nowhere.

If it was any consolation, we were getting there fast.

At most, we agreed that the key was Salerno.

All we knew—until if and when we learned more from Johnson's uncle—was that he was a Chicago lawyer who had served with Richard Hanover, had started visiting Jennifer Hanover right after her father was killed, and had her sign some kind of legal document which *may* have been opposed to Jennifer's interests.

"And why, after he had visited Jennifer with the notary and got what he needed—whatever it was for whatever reason—would he go back there again?" Darlene asked.

Before I could answer *I don't know,* the office door opened and Edward Salerno walked in.

36

"Did you take a taxi all the way out here?" I asked.

"Actually, I offered your boy Billy a C-note to run me over. He's waiting for me, I told him to keep the meter running. He tried calling your cell, to give you a heads up, but there was no answer."

"My phone ran out of juice."

"It happens. You've been asking about me and watching me for nearly a week, Diamond. What do you want from me? Mind if I sit?"

"I'm Darlene Roman," Darlene said, giving me a moment to decide what I wanted from him. "Pull up a chair."

"What's your business with Jennifer Hanover," I finally managed.

"What business is it of yours?"

"I'm trying to help a friend."

It was enough for Salerno—all he needed to hear.

"That is exactly what *I* am trying to do," he said.

And he told us about *his* friend. Richard Hanover.

"For as long as I can remember, all I wanted to do was practice the law.

"I took pre-law courses at college in Chicago, and was accepted to several law schools—but my father was a blue-collar factory worker and there was no way I could have afforded tuition. I knew the military offered tuition programs for personnel, so I joined the Marines but, before I could take advantage of the perks, I had to actively serve. I was deployed to Kuwait, where I met Richard Hanover.

"Richard and I became fast friends, and then he disappeared during a scouting mission.

"When I completed active service, I applied to and was accepted into the Marine's Judge Advocate Program. First, I needed to complete law school. The government handled the cost.

"The officer candidate course in law followed, and once completed I was sent to the Naval Justice School in Newport, Rhode Island. Then I entered the Judge Advocate General's Corps, JAG. I defended Marines accused of all types of civil, criminal and military crimes.

"When I heard Richard Hanover had resurfaced after more than ten years, and was accused of desertion and facing a court-martial, I asked to be assigned to his defense.

"It wasn't until he had returned to the states that he first learned his mother had passed away years before.

"I had absolutely no doubt Richard had been a prisoner all those years. The experiences he described to me were vivid and horrible. I am not going to repeat what Richard went through, because I don't want to hear it again. But the desertion rate among Gulf and Iraq War soldiers had risen by more than eighty percent, and the military was intent on discouraging more cases.

"It took a year for us to clear Richard, and finally secure his release.

"Soon after, I left the Marines to set up private practice in Chicago.

"With whatever money Richard had, he purchased a car. All he wanted to do was to get back to California to see his sister. He only made it as far as Ohio.

"He had stopped for a meal at a restaurant outside of Columbus. When he came back out to the parking lot, he found two men trying to break into his car. He confronted them, a struggle ensued, and one of the men was killed.

"It was clearly a case of self-defense, but Richard was arrested and he was charged with involuntary manslaughter.

"Richard called me. I couldn't help him myself, since I'm not licensed to practice law in Ohio. But I did I have a good friend, a fine lawyer, who *could* practice there. He took on Richard's case pro bono, and he bargained for an eighteen-month prison term.

"With any luck, Richard could get an early release before this Christmas.

"I had visited Richard a few times at Franklin County Correctional Center in Columbus. When I heard his father had been killed, I went down to give him the news.

"He took the news hard. I believe he still hoped for a reconciliation. But his biggest concern was what would happen to Jennifer, now that their father was gone.

"Richard desperately needed assurance that Jennifer would be taken care of. He pleaded with me to come out here and do whatever I could do to provide that assurance."

"Tragic," Darlene said.

I could have echoed her sentiment but I had a few questions I was hoping to get in before Salerno turned it back on me.

"Who else knew Richard had returned? Who may he have reached out to? Relatives? Uncle, aunt, cousins? Any of the others you served with?"

"No one."

"And who knows where Richard is now?"

"Only me, and now you, as far as I know. I doubt the Marine Corps knows where he is, and would guess they couldn't care less."

"When you informed Richard of his father's death, did he consider he might have an inheritance coming?"

"No. In Richard's own words, it was *extremely improbable.*"

"What's the nature of the document you had Jennifer sign?"

"It is an affirmation, for the record, that she has a surviving biological brother—and information on where Richard could be located. I needed both Jennifer and Richard's signatures verified. Since Richard couldn't be here, I had him sign the document when I visited him in prison and I found a notary who, for a price, was willing to bend the rules. I've told you my business with Jennifer Hanover. Tell me yours."

I gave him the whole story from the beginning.

Our guesses and misses, our mistaken suspicions—Vinnie, Bobby Lockhart, Loretta Bailey.

Salerno never interrupted.

Most of what he was hearing was news to him, since much of what we had learned was not public knowledge.

"And now," I concluded, "you have successfully eliminated our last remaining suspects."

"I have two questions," Salerno said.

"Okay."

"You seem convinced that whoever wanted Frederick Hanover dead was after his riches. Have you considered his murder may have been personally motivated? Orchestrated by someone who hated him so intensely, he or she could not tolerate seeing him alive."

We had to admit we hadn't considered it.

"What's the other question?" Darlene asked.

"Does that dog ever come out from under the desk?"

Darlene flashed her incomparable smile and answered.

"Only when he senses a threat, or when I say *do you want to go for a walk.*"

With that, Tug McGraw came out from under the desk.

"I guess I'm committed now. Can I bring you something from the delicatessen downstairs?" she asked Salerno. "The food is very good, and the coffee is not bad."

"No, thank you, but I could use a drink."

"I have George Dickel Sour Mash," I said.

"Perfect."

"I'll be back," Darlene said, and she quickly followed the dog out of the office.

I poured drinks.

"How long will you be in California?" I asked.

"Four more days. I have a court case beginning on Monday, and need to prepare. The next visiting hours are tomorrow and Saturday. I'll visit Jennifer tomorrow morning and afternoon, work on my opening statements at the hotel on Thursday and Friday, visit her Saturday morning and afternoon, and return to Chicago that evening."

"Do you plan to fill Richard in right away?"

"I won't be able to visit him until after my court case. I'll call and tell him Jennifer will be alright. I think I'll hold off on what you've told me. I believe he would be better not hearing it for a while, and not on the telephone."

"What is Jennifer like?"

"She is like a beautiful, innocent child. You should come with me to visit her before I leave."

"Let's plan on it. Saturday morning," I said, refilling our glasses.

Salerno waited for Darlene and the pooch to return, so he could tell her he enjoyed meeting her.

Who didn't.

I walked Salerno down to the street, to thank Billy and square what I owed him for the stake-out.

Billy told me I could call him anytime I need help.

I made arrangements to meet Salerno for breakfast on Saturday, and I would join him afterwards to visit Jennifer Hanover.

Back up in the office, I called Irving Sulam and told him he could go home to his family.

"What now?" Darlene asked.

"Now, we call it a day. I'll play pinochle with Romano and Fennessy this evening, and try to put it out of my mind. Tomorrow morning, I'll wake with a clearer understanding of how *nowhere* we are."

Following a late night of card playing—strictly avoiding shop talk and liberally indulging in bourbon and cigarettes—I slept like a drunken baby.

37

I woke up Wednesday morning hoping for a fresh optimistic outlook.

All I woke up with was a raging headache.

On the plus side, in fact all we had on the plus side, was that the news from Lionel Katz had been good. Vinnie would not face indictment until the San Francisco Police Department could *satisfactorily demonstrate they had done everything they could do to identify and investigate other possibilities.*

Vinnie was safe for the time being.

He was out on bail and had spent his first day at home on Tuesday.

I hadn't found an opportunity to visit Vinnie, but Darlene had while I was running around Berkeley.

Darlene confirmed my certainty.

Vinnie told her he would lose his mind if his mother didn't return to Los Angeles.

Very soon.

I had taken Bobby Lockhart's photographs from the office, with the intention of returning them to his mother on Wednesday morning.

I called Darlene and told her to expect me late.

"Did they help?" Lockhart's mother asked.

"They have given us new leads to investigate."

She still believed I was a police detective.

I didn't see any reason to confess I had misled her.

"I don't know if it's important," she said.

"What's that?"

"The last time Bobby was here he left a backpack. I was going through his things and I found this."

Margaret Lockhart handed me a small slip of paper, torn from a note pad, with the words DON'T FORGET professionally printed at the top and a handwritten address below.

I gave it a quick glance.

"We'll look into it," I said, placing the note into my pocket.

"Thank you again for trying to find out who killed my son."

"We won't give up until we have the answer."

I was fifteen minutes away from the office.

I jumped into my car, the slip of paper burning a hole in my pocket, and headed for North Beach.

I called Darlene.

"Can you check my desk, see if my book is laying around."

"Your book?"

"*David Copperfield.*"

"Give me a minute."

"It's here," Darlene said, back on the line a minute later.

"I'm on my way," I said.

"What is, Jake? You don't sound right."

"That's because I may have been wrong all along."

I walked up to Darlene's desk and handed her the note.

"What's this?"

"Margaret Lockhart found it with her son's things."

"It's an address," she said, handing it back.

"It's Frederick Hanover's address."

"Where Vinnie was shot?"

"Where Vinnie was shot. Where is the Dickens book?"

"On your desk, I had to unbury it."

"Come with me."

Darlene followed me to my desk.

I picked up the book and flipped through the pages until I found the two items that I had placed there a week ago—and had forgotten.

I placed one on the desk.

"Is that a check?"

"Yes," I said, comparing the other item against the note I had taken from Lockhart's mother. Both had the printed heading DON'T FORGET.

"What's up?"

"Do they look like they came from the same note pad?" I asked, handing her both.

"Where did this one with the phone number come from?"

"Jefferson Talbot."

"Seriously?"

"Yes."

"Are you thinking Talbot wrote both notes?"

"I don't know what to think."

Darlene studied both slips of paper.

"These are common memo pad sheets," she said, "but it wouldn't matter if they came from the same pad or not if the handwriting matches. I think we should get these over to Johnson and have their people do what they do."

"I'm reluctant."

"Why?"

"If a match can't be positively confirmed, we're back where we started. It would be tantamount to inconclusive results for a polygraph test."

"Tantamount. Nice word."

"And then it looks like another of my countless hairbrained suspicions."

"What then?"

"Are there people who do handwriting comparison analysis independent of the police?"

"Sure."

"How do we find one?"

"We call Lionel Katz."

I called Tony Carlucci instead.

I told him I needed to see Katz, at my office, as soon as possible.

I told Tony I would be extremely appreciative, avoiding the words *forever grateful.*

Carlucci called back with word that Katz was on his way.

Katz examined both slips of paper.

"Why not use the police forensics lab?"

"Whether Talbot wrote both these notes, or not, I would rather he not know we're looking at it. The police are not good at discretion."

"I don't know, Diamond," Katz said. "There are only digits on one, and none of these cell phone number digits match any in the address. I know an expert who is very accomplished and respected in handwriting analysis—and qualified to testify in court—but I'm afraid this may not be enough for him to make an irrefutable determination. If we had a better handwriting sample to compare to the handwritten address, it could make all the difference."

"How about a signature?"

"That would help."

The check for five-thousand dollars that Jefferson Talbot had written for me a week earlier was sitting on my desk.

I picked it up and handed it to Katz.

"Can we put a rush on this?" I asked.

"Sure," Katz said. "I'll let Tony and John know it's a *special order.*"

. . .

"You don't look good," Darlene said, when Katz left the office.

"I feel worse. Too much bourbon last night, and this business is wearing me down to nothing. I need to get away from this for a while, at least until we hear something from Katz. I'm going to take a handful of aspirin, hop into the Impala, drive down the coast to Monterey or to Carmel, and check into a room with a view."

"Would you like company?"

"No offense, Darlene, but I think I need to be alone."

"No offense taken, Garbo, I understand. Have you had anything to eat today?"

"No."

"It wouldn't hurt. Can I buy you lunch before you leave?"

"Sure, Darlene, you can buy me lunch."

Later, Wednesday, I sat at the shore gazing out over Monterey Bay.

I lit another cigarette and watched the sun sink into the ocean.

I spent all day Thursday doing all I could to keep my head in the clouds.

After a hearty breakfast, I drove down the coast to Big Sur.

After a long walk through the park, I soaked for an hour at Sykes Hot Springs before heading back north to Monterey.

In the evening, I treated myself to a perfectly grilled Porterhouse steak and later took a seat at the shore for an encore of the sunset.

Back in my hotel room, I finished reading *David Copperfield*.

Dicken's final chapter, "A Last Retrospective", is written in the present tense—a restatement of events in the lives of many of the major characters presented as if they were happening at the moment rather than in the past.

Despite the great amount of sadness throughout the novel, Dicken's succeeds in making it nearly all right in the end.

I fell asleep, and I dreamed of happy endings.

I started back to San Francisco at daybreak.

I had asked Darlene not to call me unless it was a *real emergency*.

So, I hadn't heard about Elizabeth Talbot until I walked into the office on Friday morning.

38

Darlene looked as if she had been sitting on the edge of her seat for two days.

"You heard from Katz?"

"Not yet."

"What's happened?"

"When you spoke with Jefferson Talbot the first time, at his office."

"Yes?"

"Do you remember when that was?"

"I don't know, a few weeks ago."

"It was exactly two weeks ago. Friday."

"Okay."

"Did he happen to mention his wife?"

"He has never mentioned his wife. What about his wife?"

"Two days before you met him, Wednesday, his wife tried to take her own life. An overdose of sleeping pills. The day Frederick Hanover was buried."

"Why wouldn't he have mentioned it? And how do you know?"

"I heard from his secretary, Molly. Talbot had noticed that the check he gave you hadn't been cashed, and asked her to call to find out if there had been any problem with it. I asked to speak to Talbot, to let him know we had simply not gotten around to it and to thank him personally. Molly told me he was out of the office, visiting his wife at Saint Mary's Hospital. Molly didn't know why his wife had been hospitalized. Do you remember Josephine Leone, the referral we got from Romano?"

"Yes."

"She is an administrator at Saint Mary's. I called her. I asked how her son Tim was doing. She said he was doing very well. He is back at home and working hard to catch up on missed schoolwork. Then I asked a favor. I told her we would totally understand if she couldn't help us for reasons of patient confidentiality—and I assured her that no one would hear about it. Josie told me Elizabeth Talbot has been in a coma since being admitted that Wednesday."

"I don't know what to make of it," I said.

"I can take a wild guess."

"Go for it."

"Elizabeth Talbot and Frederick Hanover were having an affair."

"In which case, Edward Salerno may have hit the nail on the head. A personal vendetta. A crime of passion. Talbot finds out somehow, and has Hanover murdered."

"It would certainly qualify as a motive."

"And Talbot's wife?"

"That's a trickier guess. I can imagine three scenarios. The malevolent, Talbot attempts to murder her and make it appear a suicide. The ironic, she suspects her husband is responsible for Hanover's death and it drives her to suicide."

"And?"

"The romantic. Elizabeth Talbot loved Frederick Hanover so much, she decided she couldn't live without him."

"Boy oh boy."

"That's one way of putting it. So, do we take it to Johnson?"

"We wait until we hear what Katz comes up with."

"And if the handwriting analysis comes back inconclusive?"

"Ask me again, then. Now, I need some fresh air."

. . .

I walked for several hours.

Down Columbus Avenue to Washington Street, out to the Ferry Building where I grabbed a bite.

I walked the Embarcadero up to Fisherman's Wharf and to Ghirardelli Square.

I walked to the end of the Hyde Street Pier and faced-off with the Bay—surrounded by vendors, panhandlers, performers, old men, and young women guarding small children in strollers.

I have always been drawn to large bodies of water.

Growing up in Brooklyn, I spent most summer days in the Atlantic Ocean at Coney Island.

It is the immensity, the proportion, that affects me.

Something so much bigger than any of us mere mortals.

The vastness of the sea helps me gain perspective.

I understood that the past few weeks had been about Vinnie.

If it had not been for Vinnie's situation, I likely would never have heard of Frederick Hanover or Bobby Lockhart or Loretta Bailey or Jefferson Talbot.

And I realized these people really meant little or nothing to me.

I held no admiration for Hanover.

The way he had treated his children was contemptible. And he had possibly had an affair with the wife of his partner and friend.

I did not mourn his death.

I felt empathy for Bobby Lockhart's mother—but as far as Bobby's fate itself, I felt no loss.

It had been all about Vinnie.

But now, if Jefferson Talbot had anything to do with Hanover's murder, it was about Talbot also.

If he was involved, he had been playing me all along.

Misleading me, as Bobby Lockhart had misled Vinnie.

Lockhart had crossed Vinnie.

And I now strongly suspected Talbot had crossed me.

If I were to list things I find unsavory—like runny egg yolks, raw green bell peppers, the Atlanta Braves, "Angie" by The Rolling Stones, every *Meet the Parents* movie, and anything gluten-free—random violence against innocents and double-crossing would share the top of the list.

A double-cross is particularly distasteful because it involves betrayal of trust.

And trust, which is sadly in short supply, is something I value.

I am a believer in the golden rule.

I also believe that in certain cases it could stand amendment.

Do unto others as you would have them do unto you, or be prepared to suffer the consequences.

The chicken crossed the road either to get to the other side or because the road crossed the chicken.

I walked back to the office.

"Katz called," Darlene reported.

"And?"

"His expert said he would personally bet the farm that both handwriting samples are the same, but he is not confident it would hold up in court."

"Well, I considered that possibility."

"Now what?"

"Now I pay Jefferson Talbot a visit."

"And?"

"Try to cross the road."

CROSSING THE ROAD

*Charity begins at home
and justice begins next door.*
—Charles Dickens

39

Following a university theatre program, and some success acting on off-off-Broadway stages, I relocated to California from New York with fantasies of movie stardom.

After appearing in several B-movies portraying criminal thugs who had few spoken lines and never survived past the first reel, I had to admit that my dreams were fated to be unrealized.

When I met Jimmy Pigeon, a private investigator contracted as an expert consultant on the set of one of the films, his experience and charisma inspired me to change career paths.

I abandoned the public eye to become a private eye.

In spite of the brevity of my Hollywood experiment, I was not without acting skills. Tools which have served to my advantage on many occasions.

I am not a poker player.

Poker is a gambler's game, and I've witnessed the perils of the gambling bug far too often.

Vinnie Stradivarius, and his father before him, were two sad examples.

I prefer a friendly game of pinochle.

That being said, among the many things I learned from Jimmy Pigeon was the art of bluffing.

Pigeon taught me everything he knew about that particular skill, and Jimmy knew a great deal about it.

I had convinced myself Jefferson Talbot was guilty.

Darlene agreed, and I believed Sergeant Johnson would agree also.

However, there was still not enough incontestable evidence to guarantee conviction by a jury of Talbot's peers.

It was going to take a skillful acting performance and artful bluffing to condemn Talbot.

I walked into the office of Talbot and Hanover and moved directly to the receptionist's desk.

"Hello, Molly," I said, as she looked up from her computer monitor. "Has Mr. Talbot returned from the hospital?"

It took her a moment to recognize me, which elicited a smile.

The next moment she remembered her job and why she was there.

"He has. Do you have an appointment?"

"I don't."

"Mr. Talbot prefers that visitors make an appointment."

"I'm sure he does. I'm the same way myself. But, do me a favor, Molly. Give him a jingle. Tell him Jake Diamond is here to see him, and I have the answer to the question he so generously contributed funds to investigate."

"Would you like coffee or a soft drink while you wait?"

"I won't be waiting that long."

Molly buzzed Talbot's office, took part in a short exchange, and sent me back.

"Have a seat, Jake. Am I to understand you have discovered who was behind Frederick's death?"

"Yes. But, if you will kindly bear with me, I have several questions before I get around to it."

"Certainly."

"How did you learn your wife was having an affair with Hanover?"

"What do you mean?"

Talbot shifted in his seat, and was now looking past me.

As if at someone standing at my shoulder behind me.

"It's a fairly simple question, Jeff. But wait, allow me to guess. You had suspicions and you employed a private detective who showed you photographs that tore your heart out."

"I don't know what you're talking about, and I think you should leave."

Talbot still would not look into my eyes.

Jimmy Pigeon had also taught me how to recognize a *tell*.

Talbot's reaction told me nearly all I needed to know, but did not tell me whether his investigator was a man or a woman.

I went with the percentages.

"Relax, Jeff. I'm playing with you," I said. "I know for a fact you hired a private investigator. I met him when he sought me out and sold me copies of the photographs. I suppose you didn't compensate him enough to honor the sacred oath of confidentiality or cover his vacation in Mexico. Gives us all a bad name."

"You're bluffing."

"That's not my style."

"In any case, if Elizabeth and Frederick *were* having an affair what business is it of yours?"

"Good. Now we're getting somewhere. Which brings us to the handwriting analysis."

"Again, I don't follow you."

"The address you gave Bobby Lockhart, the cell phone number you jotted down for me on the same nifty DON'T FORGET notepad, and the check for five thousand dollars. A respected expert has positively confirmed that they were all written by the same hand. And, if that isn't enough, I located an employee at the Marina Inn who will swear she saw you there on the night Loretta Bailey was killed. Motive, opportunity, eyewitness, it's all there. If I hand it all to the police you will be in custody in a flash facing charges of conspiracy to murder Frederick Hanover and Bobby Lockhart, the murder of Bailey, and possibly the attempted murder of your wife. Are you catching on yet?"

"*If* you hand it to the police?"

"There you go, Jeff. I don't care about Hanover or Lockhart or Bailey. As they say, and as I am sure you are beginning to understand, you play with fire you get burned. All I really care about, all I have cared about from the start, is my friend. Lionel Katz is an exceptional attorney, with unequaled connections and bargaining power. Katz has assured us the charges against Vinnie will be reduced to a class A misdemeanor, carrying maximum penalties of up to a five-thousand-dollar fine and up to twelve months jailtime. Katz has also assured us that he worked out a bargain with the prosecutors. A five-thousand-dollar fine and a suspended jail sentence—twelve months' probation and community service—and no felony record. Your check will cover the fine, but Vincent was very nearly killed and he has been put through a terrible ordeal. He deserves compensation. I can make everything that I have go away completely, on two conditions. Should I go on?"

"Go on," Talbot said.

"First, you fund a money market account for Vincent Stradivarius in the amount of one hundred thousand dollars. Balances subject to taxation only upon withdrawal."

"And the second condition?"

"I have to admit, Talbot, I am really enjoying this little get together. The second condition is that you turn your interest in the company entirely over to Richard and Jennifer Hanover."

"That would leave me with nothing."

"Except your freedom. Are we in business?"

Talbot lost his tongue.

"Good, I'll take that as a *yes*. I can have the appropriate legal documents prepared, all ready to be signed and witnessed, in a few hours. I'll call you on your cell phone, and we'll meet at *my* office. Meanwhile, pick up an additional five thousand in cash. For the notary. By the way, I'm curious, how did you find a complete screw-up like Bobby Lockhart?"

"He came in to see Frederick about a job with the company, thinking he could use his association with Richard Hanover as a reference. Frederick was out of town, so *I* saw Lockhart instead. He was a basket-case, a psychological disaster. I told him we would keep his application in our files in the event of a suitable opening."

"Always handy to have a psychopath on the Rolodex. And how did you get the drop on an accomplished assassin like Loretta Bailey?"

"I suppose she underestimated me."

"Don't expect me to make the same mistake."

I rose from my seat and started for the door.

"Diamond."

"Yes?" I said, stopping at the threshold.

"I didn't try to kill my wife, she attempted it herself."

"I don't care," I said.

And I left him there.

"Have a nice day," Molly said, as I passed her desk.

"Good advice," I said.

I went back to headquarters and gave Darlene the lowdown.

I had considered calling on Lionel Katz to draw up the paperwork, but I already owed the Carlucci brothers one too many.

I called Edward Salerno instead.

I gave him the what and the what for.

Salerno said he could get everything I needed over to the office by four.

I called Talbot and told him where to be and when.

Then I made the other calls.

Salerno sent the paperwork over with Tom Romano's nephew Billy and a message. He apologized for being unable to join in the festivities. He was too far behind in preparing for his upcoming court case. Salerno also asked Billy to remind me we had a date for breakfast in the morning, to be followed by a visit to meet

Jennifer Hanover.
At four, the others arrived.
We waited.

40

When Jefferson Talbot walked into our office, he was surprised to find a party of four.

I offered Talbot a chair and made the introductions.

"These are my associates, who will serve as the two required witnesses to the signing," I said, indicating Darlene and the man sitting beside her. "And the notary, Irving Sulam. You can trust their discretion. Did you bring the cash?"

Talbot handed me an envelope.

A fat envelope.

"There is a lot more than five thousand dollars here," I said.

"It's fifteen thousand. When we are done, I will need the two notes and the check. And, of course, the photographs."

"No problem. Let's do this."

After the documents had been signed and witnessed, and Irving Sulam had affixed his official seal to both, Vinnie had a hundred thousand dollars in the bank, Talbot and Hanover was the property of Frederick Hanover's children and I exhaled.

"Well that, as they say, is that."

"What about the notes, the check and the photographs?" Jefferson Talbot asked.

"I'm afraid I can't help you with the photographs."

"You said it was no problem."

"I lied. The truth is I have no photos. I never had any photos. I relied on intuition, and I got it right for a change. As far as the notes and the check are concerned, they are no longer in my possession. You'll have to talk to Sergeant Johnson about that."

Johnson rose from where he had been sitting beside Darlene, walked to the office door and ushered in two uniforms.

While one of the officers handcuffed Jefferson Talbot, Johnson did the Miranda thing.

"Take him to Vallejo Street and drop him in an interrogation room. I'll be right behind you."

"What have you done, Diamond," Talbot said, as they led him away.

"Crossed the road."

"Do you think he'll be convicted?" I asked Johnson.

"We can be much more aggressive trying to gather evidence now. We *will* find the investigator he hired, and get the photographs. And we'll energetically try to locate a witness who saw Talbot at the hotel where Bailey was murdered. Maybe, if we are really lucky, we will find the gun and the photographs when we search Talbot's home and office. In any case, the man is out of business."

"Thanks for sticking with this, for standing by Vinnie."

"You're welcome. And, Diamond."

"Yes?"

"The envelope."

"The envelope?"

"I need to bring the cash in, as evidence."

"All of it?"

"What do you mean?"

"I promised Irving five thousand for all of his trouble. And five thousand replaces the check I handed over to you and would cover Vinnie's fine."

"I'll take the remaining five. With the envelope."

Darlene removed ten thousand dollars, and she passed the envelope to Johnson.

"Thanks again," I said, as the sergeant moved to leave the office.

"Don't mention it. And I mean *don't* mention it."

After Johnson left, I handed five grand to Irving Sulam.

"Where did you get this cash?" I asked.

"What cash?"

We were alone in the office.

"Would you like to join me tomorrow, for breakfast with Edward Salerno and a visit to meet Jennifer Hanover?" I asked Darlene.

"I can't tomorrow. I promised my father we would take a ride to Stinson Beach to visit my friends and give the dog a good run. Maybe we can visit her another time, I would really like to meet her."

"I'm sure we could do that."

"What now?"

"I would offer you a drink, but all we have handy is George Dickel."

"Dickel'll do."

Over breakfast Saturday morning, I brought Salerno up to date.

"Who will run the company?" he asked.

"It pretty much runs itself. Molly said she and the two junior associates can handle things temporarily, while the business is officially renamed Hanover Enterprises. The only pressing decision is with regard to the Bayshore Heights property. But, once Richard is released, he will need to be prepared for a whole new reality. Have you spoken with him?"

"Only to let him know Jennifer will be safe and sound. Are you ready to meet her?"

"Sure."

. . .

Salerno introduced me to Jennifer as a friend of her brother.

It earned a warm reception.

She didn't talk much, but was a good listener.

I told her about what I did for a living, if you could call it a living, and how ridiculous it could be at times.

She seemed to find it extremely entertaining.

Jennifer was as lovely as Salerno had led me to expect.

She showed me some of her oil and watercolor paintings, which were exceptional.

After two hours, which flew by, a nurse came into the room.

"I need fifteen minutes alone with Jennifer," she said.

I decided it was time for me to bow out, allow the remaining time for Jennifer and Salerno.

"I will visit again," I said.

Her smile was all the thanks I needed.

Salerno walked me out to my car.

"When do you think it would be a good time to tell Richard everything?" I asked.

"As I said, I think it should be done in person. And the trial beginning Monday could tie me up for quite some time. On top of that, in my opinion, Richard should hear it from you."

"Me?"

"You'll love Columbus."

THE OTHER SIDE

*To travel hopefully is a
better thing than to arrive.*
—Robert Louis Stevenson

Following his arrest and interrogation, Jefferson Talbot was held in custody over the weekend awaiting an arraignment hearing.

His office and his home had been searched, but there was nothing found connecting him to Bobby Lockhart or to Loretta Bailey that contributed to what we already had.

No weapon.

No incriminating photos of his wife with Frederick Hanover.

Johnson sent word throughout the Bay area that police were looking for a private investigator who was hired by Talbot.

Lieutenant Folgueras in Oakland had officers speaking to every single employee at the Marina Inn, hoping someone had noticed Talbot there when Loretta Bailey was killed.

Talbot was arraigned Monday morning and released on bail.

The following day, Elizabeth Talbot passed away at St. Mary's.

She had never come out of the coma.

The same evening, police received a call reporting what sounded like a gunshot coming from a neighbor's home.

The two officers who responded found the front door of Jefferson Talbot's home wide open.

They found him in the bedroom. DOA.

Talbot had apparently put the barrel of a handgun into his mouth and pulled the trigger.

Talbot had left a note confessing all, including his business with Bobby Lockhart and Loretta Bailey. He ended the note insisting, again, that he had nothing to do with his wife's death.

It was later determined that the weapon he used to end his own life was the weapon that killed Bailey.

The news had me questioning what I might possibly say about a man whose feelings for his wife had compelled him to murder her lover—his long-time friend—and then follow her to the grave.

I could think of nothing to say about it.

Maybe there are degrees of betrayal.

Perhaps love is sometimes like a wild animal that you bring into your home to domesticate, only to find it cannot be tamed.

I couldn't say.

Nevertheless, Sergeant Johnson was confident it was *case closed*.

And Lionel Katz was positive Vinnie was off the hook.

On Wednesday, I paid a final visit to Margaret Lockhart.

Darlene along.

I told Bobby's mother that the people responsible for his death had been identified and brought to justice.

"Why was he killed?" she asked.

I didn't believe the details of her son's demise would ease her grief.

I was at a loss for words.

"Your son was in the wrong place at the wrong time, Mrs. Lockhart," Darlene said.

Thankfully, Margaret let it slide.

Darlene ran me out to the airport directly from our stop to see Lockhart's mother.

I boarded a flight to Ohio.

I sat at a table across from Richard Hanover in the visitors' hall at the Franklin County Correctional Center in Columbus.

Edward Salerno had arranged the visit, and had let Hanover know to expect me.

I told him everything.

Wrapping up with the news that he and his sister were now the proud proprietors of an extremely successful business enterprise.

I also threw in a plug for Bayshore Heights Village.

"I have received word I could be released as early the end of this month, free and clear, my debt to society paid in full. I'll be moving to California, after more than fifteen years away. My major regret is I never had the chance to see my mother again. I will visit Jennifer as soon as possible. Then, the first thing I will do in my new position will be to guarantee that the residents at Bayshore Heights are not dispossessed."

"That's very good news," I said.

"I'll admit, I'm nervous about seeing my sister after all this time."

"Believe me, there's nothing to be worried about. Call me when you're in San Francisco and you feel you're ready, and I will take you out to Berkeley to make the introductions."

I was back in San Francisco on Thursday evening.

First thing Friday morning, I went out to visit Vinnie.

Frances Stradivarius was conspicuous in her absence.

"Where's your mother?"

"She returned to Los Angeles yesterday. I suppose she felt I could take care of myself. And I'm sure she missed her twice a week bridge club. You'll never believe what I learned yesterday."

Nice segue.

"I can believe almost anything, Vin, what's up?"

"My community service will be with the Salvation Army, inventorying books for their retail outlets. How cool is that?"

"Very cool. If you come across anything by British, French or Russian novelists from the nineteenth century, maybe you can set them aside for me."

"That might be against the rules, Jake."

This from a guy who was nearly indicted for murder.

"I bet it is, Vinnie. I lost my head."

"Do you want to hear something funny, Jake?"

"What's that?"

"I'm going to miss my mother."

I'm not certain I would have called it funny, but it was definitely something.

"I want to thank you again, Jake, for everything you did to help me through this."

"It's nothing you wouldn't have done for me."

"Except you would never get yourself into that kind of jam."

"You never know, Vin, you just never know."

Darlene was already busy at work when I made it to the office.

I would have asked what she was up to, but I really didn't need to know and would probably not have understood.

There was a lot Darlene did for Diamond Investigations that was over my head.

I told her about my visit with Richard Hanover.

"What is he like?"

"He is a man who has been told for a very long time that he is unworthy, and who is finally able to consider he is actually a good man with much better days ahead."

"A happy ending?"

I wondered for an instant what David Copperfield would have thought.

"Could be."

"Can you do me a favor?" Darlene asked.

"Name it."

"I've been invited to go skiing in Colorado over the weekend."

I was tempted to ask why anyone would want to do that, but I held my tongue.

"You would like me to take care of the pooch."

"My dad will tend to Tug McGraw. The sink in the bathroom is leaking badly."

The challenges of running a business.

"I wouldn't know where to begin."

"I'm aware of that. I've scheduled a plumber for tomorrow morning at ten. Someone will need to be here when he arrives."

"That I can handle."

"Great. I need to get out of here, we're leaving this afternoon. I'll be back Monday morning."

"Have a good time," I said, "and try to avoid trees at all costs."

After Darlene beat it, I called Johnson.

"I was wondering..." I said, not sure how to phrase the request.

"Are you going to tell me," Johnson said, after a few seconds of silence, "or would you like me to guess?"

"The Bailey investigation should be wrapped up and in the books."

"If that's a question, yes."

"Since there will be no trial for Talbot, how soon would evidence from the Bailey case be released?"

"That would be up to the Oakland Police Department. Are you looking for a souvenir?"

"There *is* something I *would* like, if possible. Could you possibly appeal to Folgueras in Oakland?"

I told him what I was hoping to do.

"I'll give it my best shot," Johnson said.

"Thanks."

"And, Diamond."

"Yes?"

"Keep a tight leash on your boy Vinnie. Discourage him from betting on cards or horses or ball games or elections. He got real lucky this time, but his propensity for bad luck is legendary."

"I have been trying to keep Vinnie Strings out of trouble for a very long time."

"Try harder."

All of the talk about mothers lately—Richard Hanover's mother, Bobby Lockhart's mother, Vinnie's mom—had me thinking about Mary.

I picked up the telephone.

"Jacob?" my mother said.

Good guess.

"Yes."

"What a surprise."

Although Mary Falco Diamond represented the Italian-American, Roman Catholic side of my heritage—she had the Jewish mother guilt thing down cold.

"I'd like to take you out to dinner on Sunday."

"Don't be foolish. I'll cook. Will Darlene be joining us?"

"Darlene will be out of town."

"Would you rather wait until she returns?"

I had to give myself credit.

Planning a get together with Mary without Darlene on hand as a buffer was very courageous.

"No need, Sunday would be great."

"I'm sorry Darlene will be unavailable. But in that case, I can make my gravy with meatballs, sausage and braciola."

Thus, the upside.

"That's a lot of work, Mom. It will take a lot of time."

"Time is one thing I have a lot of," Mary said.

And there it was again.

On Saturday morning, I watched as a plumber skillfully replaced a leaking faucet.

"Do you like your work?" I asked.

"It pays the bills. How about your work?"

"Sometimes."

"Sometimes you like it?"

"Sometimes it pays the bills."

A week later, I received word from Edward Salerno that Richard Hanover would be released in nine days—and Richard planned on giving me a call once he had settled into his new residence at the family home and his new office.

The following day Sergeant Johnson called.

"Talk about pulling teeth. Folgueras was finally able to free what you're after from evidence. He's having it sent over sometime later today. It should definitely be here by morning if you care to swing by and pick it up."

"Does Folgueras drink?"

"He's a police lieutenant, of course he drinks."

"I'll send him a bottle."

"Make sure it's Baluarte Reposado one-hundred-percent agave tequila."

I walked into the office of Hanover Enterprises with a bubble-wrapped package under my arm.

Molly was at her desk.

She was all smiles, uninterrupted by any sudden changes of demeanor.

"I suppose you've heard that Richard Hanover will be arriving in a week or so."

"I have. I must admit I'm a bit nervous."

"Don't be. He is very likeable and respectable. Though, he may need help getting acclimated."

"I can do that," Molly said.

"Listen. I brought something for him. Sort of a housewarming gift. I was hoping I could leave it for him."

"He'll be using his father's office. You can leave it there."

She escorted me to the office.

There was a shiny new nameplate on the door.

She ushered me in.

I stood looking around the room for a few moments.

"Would you like to be alone?" Molly asked.

"Not at all. I would like you to see this."

I carefully unwrapped the package, and buried the bubble-wrap in my jacket pocket.

"It's beautiful."

"It was his mother's. How about right here?" I said, gently placing the angel figurine on Richard's desk.

J.L. ABRAMO was born and raised in the seaside paradise of Brooklyn, New York on Raymond Chandler's fifty-ninth birthday.

A long-time journalist, educator and theatre artist, Abramo earned a Bachelor of Arts degree in Sociology and Education at The City College of The City University New York and a Master's Degree in Social Psychology from The University of Cincinnati.

Abramo is the author of *Catching Water in a Net*, winner of the St. Martin's Press/Private Eye Writers of America prize for Best First Private Eye Novel; the subsequent Jake Diamond Novels: *Clutching at Straws*, *Counting to Infinity* and *Circling the Runway* (Shamus Award Winner); *Chasing Charlie Chan*, a prequel to the Jake Diamond series; and the crime novels *Gravesend*, *Brooklyn Justice* and *Coney Island Avenue*.

www.jlabramo.com
www.facebook.com/jlabramo

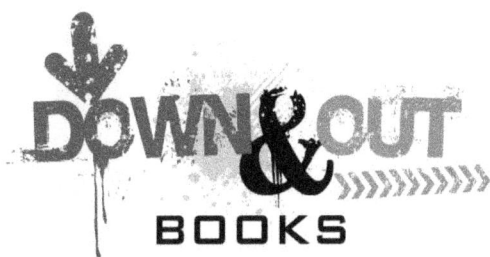

On the following pages are a few
more great titles from the
Down & Out Books publishing family.

For a complete list of books and to
sign up for our newsletter,
go to DownAndOutBooks.com.

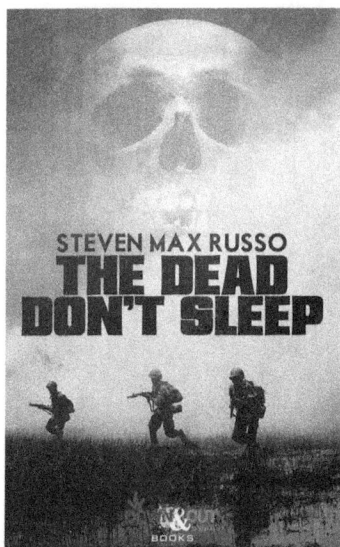

The Dead Don't Sleep
Steven Max Russo

Down & Out Books
November 2019
978-1-64396-051-7

Frank Thompson, a recent widower and aging Vietnam veteran, is down from Maine visiting his nephew in New Jersey. While at a trap range, they have a chance encounter with a strange man who claims to remember Frank from the Vietnam war.

Frank was part of a psychopathic squad of killers put together by the CIA and trained by Special Forces to cause death and mayhem during the war. That chance encounter has put three man on the squad on a collision course with the man who trained them to kill, in a nostalgic blood lust to hunt down and eliminate the professional soldier who led them all those years ago.

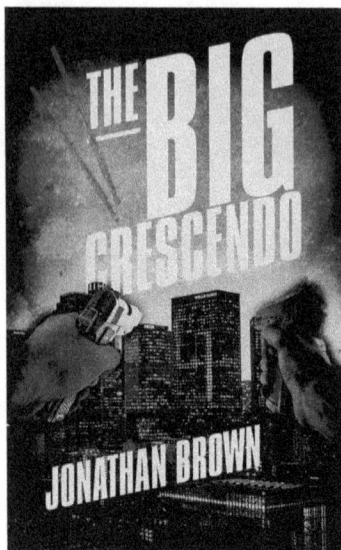

The Big Crescendo
Jonathan Brown

Down & Out Books
November 2019
978-1-64396-048-7

Lou Crasher is a wise cracking, drummer turned P.I. Drop dead gorgeous vocalist Angela, gets her musical instruments stolen. Lou vows to find them. He manages to uncover a gear-theft ring, a deadly drug cartel and accepts a risky offer from a big time music producer.

Lou's got one shot to get the gear, the girl and live to drum another day.

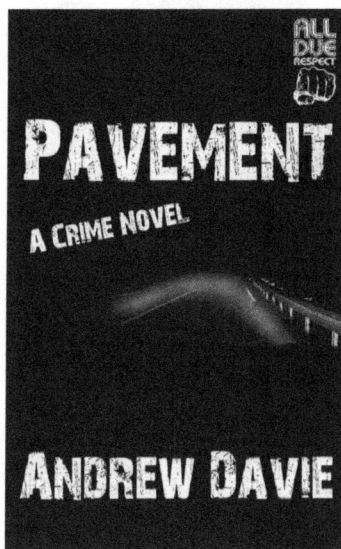

Pavement
Andrew Davie

All Due Respect, an imprint of
Down & Out Books
978-1-948235-99-0

McGill and Gropper are unlicensed private investigators who operate out of a diner and do whatever it takes to get a job done.

When a trucker attacks a prostitute, her pimp turns to McGill and Gropper for protection.

But taking the job means crossing dangerous and well-connected criminals who will stop at nothing to settle the score.

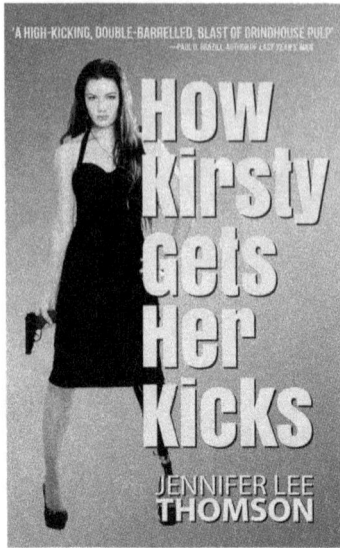

How Kirsty Gets Her Kicks
Jennifer Lee Thomson

Shotgun Honey, an imprint of
Down & Out Books
July 2019
978-1-64396-005-0

A tale of skullduggery set on the mean streets of Glasgow…

One-legged barmaid Kirsty is in a shit-load of trouble after she kills one of gangster Jimmy McPhee's goons with a stiletto heel to the head and goes on the run with a safe load of stolen cash, a hot gun and choirboy barman Jamie.